The Allergen-Free Baker's Handbook

THE *Allergen-Free* BAKER'S HANDBOOK

How to bake without gluten,
wheat, dairy, eggs, soy, peanuts,
tree nuts, and sesame

CYBELE PASCAL

CELESTIAL ARTS

Berkeley

For my two dear sons, Lennon and Montgomery

Copyright © 2009 by Cybele Pascal
Foreword © 2009 by Robert Eitches, MD
Photographs copyright © 2009 by Chugrad McAndrews

Published in the United States by Celestial Arts, an imprint of the Crown Publishing Group, a division of Random House, Inc., New York.
www.crownpublishing.com
www.tenspeed.com

Celestial Arts and the Celestial Arts colophon are registered trademarks of Random House, Inc.

Library of Congress Cataloging-in-Publication Data is on file with the publisher

ISBN 978-1-58761-348-7

Printed in China

Design by Betsy Stromberg
Food styling by Karen Shinto
Prop styling by Leigh Noe

10 9 8 7 6 5 4 3 2 1

First Edition

CONTENTS

FOREWORD **vii**

INTRODUCTION: The Whole Baker's Basket **1**

1 ▪ STOCKING YOUR ALLERGEN-FREE PANTRY **5**

2 ▪ HOW TO BAKE ALLERGEN-FREE **15**

3 ▪ MUFFINS, SCONES, BISCUITS, QUICK BREADS, AND COFFEE CAKES **23**

4 ▪ COOKIES **53**

5 ▪ CAKES **89**

6 ▪ PIES, TARTS, CRISPS, CRUMBLES, COBBLERS, PUDDINGS, BETTIES, AND BUCKLES **123**

7 ▪ YEASTED BAKED GOODS AND SAVORIES **157**

Resources **177**

Recipes Made without Refined Sugar **183**

Index **184**

Acknowledgments **189**

FOREWORD

first learned about food allergies when I was six years old. The family that lived across the street had four children; the youngest was nicknamed "Eggs." I didn't know who first called him Eggs; all I knew was that he couldn't eat eggs and that he was constantly itching his arms and legs, which were covered with thick, scary-looking skin that scabbed. I didn't know anybody else like that; in fact, I was actually more familiar with kids with polio. It wasn't until I was a third-year medical student working in pediatric dermatology that I saw a second person with food allergies. Three years later, when I worked in the Bronx during my residency, I saw more cases of food allergy, mostly in children rushed to the emergency room with hives or wheezing after eating a food they were allergic to.

After moving to California, I seemed to see such cases even more frequently. During my first week of training in allergy and immunology at UCLA, I was asked to consult on an eleven-month-old boy from Arizona who weighed only ten pounds. He looked malnourished and had a rash around his mouth. My attending professor suspected child neglect or abuse, and we all expected him to thrive within days of being in the hospital. Time passed and he remained ill, with vomiting and diarrhea to boot. I checked up on him while a nurse was feeding him a cow's milk–based formula from a sippy cup. He knocked the cup over and the formula poured onto his legs. Red blisters formed where the milk had spilled. At this point it became clear that he was allergic to the very milk with which we were trying to nourish him back to health. We stopped all forms of dairy and took him off all meds. Within forty-eight hours he was a different kid—no vomiting, happier disposition, clearer skin, and increased appetite. He returned to the clinic two months later on no medications and was unrecognizable, weighing twenty-one pounds with no skin rashes.

These anecdotes show different manifestations of food allergy, and they illustrate how food allergy, once an esoteric condition, is becoming much more prevalent. The nation has seen a mysterious rise since the 1990s in the number of children with food allergies, now estimated to be three million, or one in every twenty-five children. In the past decade alone, the prevalence has increased by 18 percent. Being a busy allergist "in the trenches," I diagnose five or more new food allergy cases each week.

So why are food allergies rising? There's no good answer, but a lot of decent guesses. One theory is that we get exposed to nuts or other foods too early. I can remember well how some children with severe food allergies had mothers who ate large quantities of that same food while pregnant and while nursing. Could in utero exposure be the culprit?

For years, allergists have been recommending that allergenic foods be introduced to children at a later age to reduce the risk of allergy. However, a 2008 study of British children found that early exposure to peanuts actually lowered the risk of future peanut allergies.

Another theory explaining the increase in food allergies is that food in the United States is processed differently. For example, there is a much higher peanut allergy rate in the United States than in China; in the United States, peanuts are mostly dry roasted while in China they are mostly boiled, which decreases the amount of the allergenic protein in the peanut. Also, the processing of peanut butter in the United States involves whipping it to prevent the oil from layering out of the solid fraction; this spreads more of the peanut protein into the oil and may result in more peanut allergies. Another theory is that some people are actually allergic to the mold that grows in peanuts, and not the peanut itself.

There is also speculation that the increasing prevalence of food allergy is related to the increase in the amount of our food that is genetically engineered. One study examined a group of people who seemed to develop a new "soy allergy" even though they had previously tolerated soy products.

It was discovered that the new allergy was only to soy that was genetically engineered from Brazil nut protein. Sure enough, all the affected people had severe Brazil nut allergy.

Whatever the reason, it is undeniable that the number of people with food allergies is on the steep rise. From a scientific point of view, allergies are the result of the body launching an exaggerated immune response against a particle it recognizes as foreign. We evolved this response to fight off infection, but the allergic immune system is so sensitive that it reacts to proteins in foods as though they were viruses. The body attempts to

destroy the foreign protein by releasing histamine, prostaglandins, and leukotrienes. These chemicals are responsible for the symptoms of an allergic reaction. These symptoms, which usually occur almost immediately after exposure to the problematic food, can vary in intensity from a little itch on the tongue or skin to full-blown anaphylaxis, a swelling in the throat and lung airways that may be life-threatening. Allergies can also present with hives, a total body rash, vomiting, diarrhea, shortness of breath, wheezing, and shock, with a severe drop in blood pressure, loss of consciousness, a lack of air exchange, and ultimately, a heart arrhythmia.

Although everyone knows that food allergies run in families, surprisingly, different family members are often allergic to different foods. And it happens that only a few foods are responsible for the great majority of food allergies. In fact, only eight foods account for more than 90 percent of all food-allergic reactions. These are milk, eggs, peanuts, tree nuts (walnuts, cashews, and so on), fish, shellfish, soy, and wheat.

These two concepts underlie the elegance and relevance of an allergy cookbook. By featuring recipes that omit all of the least-tolerated foods, a family can share these meals even if one child has a peanut allergy and another has a soy allergy and the celiac neighbor comes over with his lactose-intolerant girlfriend. As a well-known chef and the mother of a food allergy–ridden boy, Cybele Pascal is uniquely qualified to develop recipes that meet all the common food restrictions without compromising any taste. In 2006 she wrote the popular *Whole Foods Allergy Cookbook* that reinvented all our favorite home-cooked foods minus the common allergens. I consider this to be the best collection of recipes for people with food allergies, and my patients and colleagues all seem to agree. It is user-friendly with real-life stories, and best of all, the food tastes great. Pascal now follows up that meal of a book with this dessert, the answer to the child in all of us who wants to eat his cake, too.

This new book could not have come at a better time. Now, those of us with food restrictions won't have to sacrifice our favorite treats. Families will be able to eat together, sharing the same foods. And children will not be forbidden that slice of birthday cake.

Pascal has embarked on a formidable task: to bake that cake without wheat, milk, or eggs. To be able to pull that one off, as she has, is exemplary. Kudos to you, Cybele.

— **Robert Eitches, MD, FAAAAI,** assistant clinical professor at the David Geffen School of Medicine at UCLA, attending physician at Cedars-Sinai Medical Center in Los Angeles, and head of the Allergy Foundation Medical Group

INTRODUCTION

THE WHOLE *Baker's Basket*

This book is for everyone. It's for all of you out there who've ever had to say, "No thanks, I can't eat that, I'm allergic to _____." It's for anyone with food allergies or intolerances, for people with celiac disease, those on GF/CF diets, vegans, those wanting cholesterol-free baked goods and baked goods without hydrogenated fat, people wanting alternatives to refined sugar, and those who want wholesome, delicious, decadent baked goods that are free from additives, preservatives, artificial flavors, and artificial colors.

So what *is* in this cookbook, if it excludes all that? Dairy-free, soy-free chocolate chips and chocolate chunks, pure vanilla extract, sprinkles, decorating sugar, SunButter, raisins, molasses, brown sugar, cinnamon, and just about every other classic baking ingredient you can imagine. And all without the use of wheat flour, butter, or eggs! Yes, it is possible. A whole book full of yummy, *normal* baked goods that can be fed to just about anyone, no matter what his or her specific dietary needs.

This book is a baker's basket full of allergen-free versions of all your traditional favorites: muffins, scones, biscuits, quick breads, cakes, cookies, pies, tarts, crumbles, buckles, betties, and more. Every single recipe is made without wheat, dairy, peanuts, tree nuts, egg, soy, fish, shellfish, sesame, and gluten. Although the majority of these treats are made with traditional sweeteners, 30 percent of them are made with natural unrefined sweeteners, such as agave nectar, for those seeking healthy alternatives to refined sugar. For those seeking nutrient-dense baked goods, I've included recipes made with the newer gluten-free flours on the market, such as protein-packed sorghum and quinoa. For those who don't like sweets, there's a whole chapter of savories. There's something in this basket for everyone, food allergic or not, so that all the kids (or kids inside us) who've ever been the one with the "weird" food will feel like they're finally included, and can dig their hands deep inside the cookie jar.

And believe me, I know firsthand just how many of our children have experienced that alienation. My son Lennon was diagnosed with severe dairy and soy allergies in his first four months of life, and our family was thrust headfirst into the confusing, confounding, and rapidly expanding world of food allergies. When Lennon was diagnosed in 2002, food allergies were still "off the radar," but in the years that followed, the number of people in the United States with food allergies has now climbed to more than twelve million. Three million of them are children (about one in twenty-five kids has a food allergy). These rates are double what they were a decade ago. Clearly, this is a matter of increasing urgency and one that has hit the mainstream. For so many of us, food allergies are a part of our everyday life.

Given these rising numbers of food-allergic people, it's wonderful that companies such as Enjoy Life and Cherrybrook Kitchen have emerged with ready-made treats and baking mixes. But they can only make so many products, leaving those of us with food allergies feeling, well, rather short-changed. Our list of choices has heretofore been limited by what these fantastic companies can turn out. What about the hundreds of other baked items that we *crave*? What about allergen-free muffins, scones, quick breads, pies, tarts, and freshly baked bread? Unless you're lucky enough to live next to an allergen-free bakery, you've just had to do without.

But necessity is the mother of invention, right? Out of lemons you make lemonade! I dabbled with allergen-free baking in my first cookbook (*The Whole Foods Allergy Cookbook*), but have since embraced it with a passion. They say cooking is an art form, baking is science. Well, allergen-free baking is a little of both. It is most certainly an exacting science getting batters to

bind without gluten, rise without eggs, taste rich without butter, or taste sweet without sugar. But it's also uncharted territory, leaving the doors wide open for creative expression. I love baking, but in particular, I love allergen-free baking. Perhaps it's the challenge of learning to bake "without" that ultimately inspires me the most. It has opened up a wealth of new ideas and flavors that are delicious *and* safe for those with food allergies and intolerances; but if you don't want to let on that these treats are "special," nobody ever has to know.

I hope you will find baking these recipes as satisfying as I do and that they provide you with

templates to create your own allergen-free goodies to share, because it is the act of sharing and nurturing that is most satisfying of all. I love baking for people who haven't had a good cake in literally years because they can't eat gluten or dairy. And I love baking for people who aren't on restrictive diets and watching their faces light up with delighted wonder that a vegan, wheat-free, dairy-free, egg-free dessert could taste so sublime that it's often yummier than its traditional counterpart. I've converted my entire neighborhood. The better part of Laurel Canyon in Los Angeles has helped me taste-test this book. But my best and favorite taste-testers are my two sons, Lennon and Monte. If I get the "thumbs up!" from them, I know I'm good to go.

We still have food allergies in my family. Lennon, now seven, has outgrown his dairy and soy allergies, but has since been diagnosed with allergies to shellfish, tree nuts, and kiwi (in addition to just about every environmental allergen possible!). I, too, have discovered new food allergies (not surprising, given that allergies run in families). After a weeklong case of severe total body hives, I finally got myself over to Tower Allergy and Asthma at Cedars-Sinai Medical Center in Los Angeles, where the excellent Robert Eitches, MD, and Maxine Baum, MD, practice. Through testing, we confirmed that I'm allergic to certain tree nuts, fish, and shellfish, and to a lesser extent wheat, yeast, stone fruits (peaches, apricots, and so on, which interestingly enough are related to almonds), citrus fruits, and pineapple. My husband then went to Tower Allergy and Asthma, and he, too, was finally diagnosed with a long-suspected allergy to dairy, in addition to nearly every environmental allergen on the planet. The only member of my family who is not a hyperallergic individual is my son Monte. Yet, he too suffers from allergic asthma, and when it flares, he must stay away from dairy. And so, you see, we avoid a lot of foods at my house. As an adult, I'm okay with that. But kids with food allergies just want to feel *normal*. I can't tell you how many times I've been asked by my son Lennon, "When can I eat that?" Well, if it's baked goods they're asking for, the answer is "*Now!*"

1

STOCKING YOUR
Allergen-Free PANTRY

The first step to allergen-free baking is stocking your pantry. The following ingredients are the essentials of an allergen-free kitchen. Although some of them may seem foreign at first, they will quickly become familiar and easy to use. Most of these items can be found at your local health food store or natural foods market. I do almost all my pantry shopping at Whole Foods. If you do not have access to a local natural foods market, you can order necessary items online (see the Resources section on page 177) and have them shipped to you. This is also a great idea if you are buying items in bulk, which is less expensive.

The Dry Goods Pantry

Agave nectar—A lightly floral, nutritive unrefined sweetener that is suitable for diabetics, because it is low on the glycemic index. I prefer to use "light" agave nectar in my baking, but let your own taste guide you.

Amaranth flour—High-fiber, high-protein flour that adds a nutty flavor to baked goods.

Amaranth, whole grain—An old-world cereal grain that can be eaten like rice. It adds nice texture in baked goods such as quick breads.

Applesauce—Organic and unsweetened.

Baking powder—I use "double-acting" baking powder, because it has a double rise, the first when it is combined with liquid ingredients, and a second when it is heated. Double-acting baking powder also tends to stay potent longer when kept on the shelf. Most commonly sold baking powder actually is double-acting these days, but check the label to make sure. Look for gluten-free brands.

Baking soda—A common leavening agent. Baking soda reacts as soon as it is combined with an acidic ingredient and is moistened, so usually, it's best to get batters containing baking soda directly into the oven.

Baking spray—Canola oil baking spray is great for oiling pans. Many brands contain soy lecithin, however. If this is a problem for you, substitute plain canola oil.

Better Than Milk rice milk powder—A vegan milk powder that is great used anywhere you'd traditionally use powdered milk/dried milk powder.

Brown rice flour, superfine—Perhaps the most important ingredient in your allergen-free pantry.

Authentic Foods Brown Rice Flour, Superfine, is by far the superior product, producing the most tender baked goods. However, if potential cross-contamination with nut flours is a risk for you, see Resources on page 177 for brands manufactured in dedicated allergen-free facilities.

Buckwheat flour—Despite its name, there's no wheat in buckwheat. Buckwheat is an old-world gluten-free grain that adds a distinctive, rich, earthy flavor to baked goods. It is denser than most other flours, and is generally best mixed with a milder flour to balance it.

Canola oil—A mild, neutral-flavored oil that is great for baking. In my quest to find a vegetable oil that is free of any risk of cross-contamination with allergenic oils such as peanut, tree nut, soy, or sesame oil, the only one I have been able to find (other than olive oil) with a safety assurance is Crisco canola oil. See Resources on page 177 for their allergen statement.

Chocolate—Unsweetened baking chocolate (if you can't eat chocolate, or prefer not to, you may substitute unsweetened carob, but please note, these recipes have not been tested with carob; therefore, I can't guarantee the results).

Chocolate bars—Enjoy Life makes Rice Milk Chocolate Bars, Dark Chocolate Bars, and Crispy Rice Milk Bars. Also look for dairy-free, soy-free, tree nut–free unsweetened chocolate baking bars (see Resources, page 177).

Chocolate chips—Dairy-free, soy-free, gluten-free semisweet chocolate chips. I recommend Enjoy Life brand chips.

Cider vinegar—A gluten-free vinegar made from apple cider.

Cocoa powder, unsweetened—I use natural, unsweetened cocoa powder in these recipes, *not* Dutch-processed or alkalized unsweetened cocoa powder, which is treated with an alkali to neutralize its acids. Natural, unsweetened cocoa powder gives a deep chocolate flavor to baked goods. Using natural cocoa (an acid) in recipes that also include baking soda (an alkali) creates a leavening action that helps the batter rise when placed in the oven.

Popular brands are Hershey's, Ghirardelli, and Scharffen Berger. (See Resources, page 177, for Hershey's allergen statement.)

Coconut—I use unsweetened coconut flakes and unsweetened shredded coconut.

Coconut milk—Coconut milk is a sweet, creamy vegan "milk" derived from the meat of a mature coconut. It is excellent in place of dairy cream,

COCONUT AND GLUTEN-FREE OATS

I have included two ingredients in this book that need to be addressed: coconut and gluten-free oats.

I do not consider coconut a tree nut, and neither does the Food Allergy & Anaphylaxis Network (FAAN) or the American Academy of Allergy, Asthma & Immunology (AAAAI). Dr. Hugh Sampson, professor of pediatrics and chief of the division of allergy and immunology in the department of pediatrics at the Mount Sinai School of Medicine in New York City, where he also serves as director of the Jaffe Food Allergy Institute, says, "Coconut is not a nut but the seed of a drupaceous fruit. We have not restricted our nut allergic patients of coconut, and have not seen a problem. If there is any question about coconut reactivity, we test for it and occasionally have found a coconut allergic patient." However, in 2006 the FDA began mandating that coconut be considered a tree nut for labeling purposes. No one is sure how they came to this conclusion, and several food industry sources are asking them to revise this classification. As FAAN notes, coconut allergies are exceedingly rare. The available medical literature documents only a small number of allergic reactions to coconut, and most occurred in people who were not allergic to other tree nuts. Therefore, I have used coconut in a few of the recipes in this book. I don't think it's fair to deprive people of such a

healthful and delicious ingredient because the FDA has erroneously classified a fruit as a nut. But please err on the side of caution, and ask your doctor if you need to avoid coconut before making a coconut recipe.

Now, about gluten-free oats. Oats have long been a source of controversy in the gluten-free community because there is so often cross-contamination with other grains that do contain gluten, such as wheat, rye, and barley. Oats themselves are not the offender, but rather cross-contamination. I am not recommending that you bake with any old oats if you have celiac disease or are gluten intolerant. I am only recommending *certified gluten-free* oats. Over the past decade, research has shown that most people who are gluten intolerant can consume oats if other grains have not contaminated them. And thankfully, it is now possible to buy gluten-free oats from specialized vendors and growers who dedicate fields and equipment to producing oats, and oats alone. If you cannot find gluten-free oats in a store near you, order them online. (See Resources, page 177.) Amazon.com is also a great source for ordering many of the specialty items in this book, and will allow you to buy in bulk, which is much cheaper in the long run! And, as always, please play it safe. Ask your doctor if it's okay for you to bake with gluten-free oats before trying any of the oat recipes.

and adds richness to baked goods. It is sold in cans. Look for organic coconut milk without sulfites.

Corn flour—A mild, fine-grained flour that is more delicate than cornmeal. You can usually find it in health food stores or natural foods stores.

Cornmeal—Dried corn ground to fine, medium, or course texture. Cornmeal is available in yellow, white, and blue. I generally bake with fine yellow cornmeal, because I find it produces the most tender crumb.

Cornstarch, organic, GMO-free—A versatile starch that is great used in baking and in sauces. It's a thickening and binding agent. Potato starch and tapioca starch can generally be substituted one for one if you can't eat corn products.

Corn syrup, dark karo—Dark karo is made without high-fructose corn syrup; see Resources on page 177 for GMO-free brands.

Crispy rice cereal—A gluten-free cereal made from oven-toasted rice. I prefer crispy brown rice cereal, made from whole grains, which is a great innovation over the old fiberless version I grew up on.

Date sugar—A whole food sugar that can be used like brown sugar. It is much drier, however, and does not have crystals, so bear this in mind if you are substituting it for brown sugar or maple sugar. It will not dissolve or caramelize in the same way.

Decorating sugar—Great for topping cupcakes and cookies. Look for brands made with natural dyes, such as turmeric (see Resources, page 177).

Dried fruits—Apricots, cherries, cranberries, currants, dates, figs, raisins, and so on.

Egg replacer—I recommend Ener-G egg replacer. Please note that "egg substitute" is not the same thing as "egg replacer." Egg substitute often contains egg whites, and is therefore not suitable for vegans or those with egg allergies.

Flaxseed and flaxseed meal—Flaxseed and flaxseed meal are rich in omega-3s. Flaxseed meal mixed with hot water can stand in for eggs in vegan baking. You can buy preground flaxseed meal or grind your own. Store it in the fridge or freezer, or it will go rancid quickly.

Food coloring—Look for natural brands such as Seelect (see Resources, page 177).

Garfava and/or chickpea flour—A high-fiber, high-protein, gluten-free bean flour.

Gluten-free oats—There are now certified gluten-free oats available, opening up new baking options for people on gluten-free diets.

Hemp milk—A healthful alternative to rice milk for those seeking vegan, soy-free milk.

Herbs and spices—Particularly cinnamon, nutmeg, ground ginger, ground cloves, cumin, and cardamom.

Jams and jellies—Peach, apricot, strawberry, raspberry, seedless red and black currant, marion blackberry, and bitter orange marmalade are all great to have on hand for tortes, tarts, and cookie baking.

Maple sugar—An unrefined sweetener made from maple syrup. It is fabulous anywhere you'd traditionally use brown sugar.

Maple syrup—A great alternative to refined sugar.

Millet flour—A mild gluten-free flour that is great for breadmaking. It helps mimic the flavor of whole wheat flour.

Molasses—A rich, nutritive, unrefined sweetener.

Olive oil—Great for savory baked goods, and can be used in place of canola oil if it's a very mild-flavored olive oil.

Pineapple, canned, chunks, and crushed—Pineapple can be used to mimic the richness of eggs and as part of the liquid-to-sweetener ratio in baking. Try crushed pineapple in muffins and cakes. It also makes a good filling between cakes, or can be cooked into a sauce to spoon over sponge cake or shortcake.

Potato starch (not the same as potato flour)—A great thickening agent, and in gluten-free baking, it creates a tender crumb.

Prune purée (baby food)—A wonderful binder in chocolate baked goods.

Pumpkin purée, canned—Pumpkin is a great source of beta-carotene, and is fabulous baked into muffins, quick breads, and of course, pumpkin pie.

Quinoa flakes—A hot cereal that is great used anywhere you'd traditionally use old-fashioned oats.

Quinoa flour—Quinoa is a complete protein, so it packs in the nutrients in baked goods. It blends well with corn flour and cornmeal.

Rice flour—Superfine brown rice flour (the predominant ingredient in my baking flour mix) and sweet rice flour.

Rice milk—A light, delicate, plant-based milk that is great for baking. Look for gluten-free brands. I use original flavored rice milk because it's milder, but if you prefer vanilla, you may use it instead.

Salt—Fine-grained sea salt, coarse sea salt, kosher salt, and table salt. (I use fine-grained sea salt because it is more nutritive than table salt, but they are interchangeable, so feel free to use table salt, unless otherwise specified.)

Sorghum flour, sweet, white—A lightly sweet protein-rich flour that is great paired with millet flour in gluten-free bread products.

Sucanat—Unrefined dehydrated cane juice that can be used one for one as a replacement for refined sugar. Unlike with refined sugar, however, nothing has been removed from Sucanat, so it has a slight molasses flavor and is a good source of iron and potassium.

Sugar—Granulated sugar, confectioners' sugar (look for organic vegan confectioners' sugar), caster sugar (very fine), light brown sugar, and brown sugar.

Sunflower seed butter (aka SunButter), crunchy and smooth—SunButter can be used in all the ways you'd traditionally use nut butters. It is also nutritionally superior to peanut butter.

Sunflower seeds—Sunflower seeds are considered one of the world's healthiest foods. They are very rich in vitamins E and B (thiamin). In recent years, they have been touted as a great substitute for peanuts and tree nuts for those with food allergies.

Sweet potato purée, canned—Another one of nature's healthiest foods, sweet potatoes can be used like fruit purées to bind baked goods, add richness and sweetness, and keep them moist. Pumpkin purée and sweet potato purée are often interchangeable. Kids who won't eat other vegetables will often gobble down sweet potatoes.

Tapioca flour (also called tapioca starch)—A mild, starchy flour that is extremely versatile and features prominently in both of my flour mixes.

Tapioca, instant—Tapioca pudding is a tasty treat, but instant tapioca is also a great binder in fruit pies. Use it in place of cornstarch, following the instructions on the box.

Vanilla extract—Look for one of the many wheat-free, gluten-free brands on the market.

Vegan gelatin (vegan jel)—Traditional gelatin is derived from the collagen inside animals' skin and bones, which really grosses me out. Vegan gelatin can be used anywhere you'd use traditional gelatin, and is made with vegetable gum instead. It's a no-brainer, as far as I'm concerned.

Vegetable shortening, dairy-free, soy-free—I recommend Spectrum Naturals Organic Vegetable Shortening. All recipes in this book have been tested with this brand. It is the most consistent and stable of the dairy-free, soy-free vegetable shortenings on the market. It has been around the longest, and they've really perfected it to be an outstanding baking ingredient. Other brands, such as Whole Foods 365, tend to be unstable, and cause cookies, crusts, and frostings to be too soft and spread too much. If you choose to use a brand other than Spectrum, you may wish to add more flour mix to help bind the dough or batter. To do so, add 1 tablespoon at a time, until you've achieved the desired consistency. For frostings, add more confectioners' sugar, 1 tablespoon at a time.

Xanthan gum—The be-all and end-all of gluten-free baking. I don't know what we would do without it. It is a plant gum that mimics gluten. It provides structure and elasticity. A little bit goes a long way, so measure it carefully. I have found there is variation between brands. I like Ener-G's xanthan gum best. It is a derivative of corn. If you can't eat corn, you may use guar gum instead, but please note, these recipes have not been tested with guar gum.

Yeast—Rapid-rise yeast is best for gluten-free baking.

The Perishable Goods Pantry

- **Applesauce** (refrigerate after opening)
- **Berries**: assorted fresh and frozen
- **Carrots**
- **Flax meal** (refrigerate after opening)
- **Fresh herbs** (rosemary, thyme, basil, etc.)
- **Fruits**: assorted fresh and frozen
- **Gingerroot**
- **Lemons**
- **Limes**
- **Potatoes** (do not store in refrigerator)
- **Rice milk** (refrigerate after opening)
- **Sweet potatoes** (do not store in refrigerator)
- **Yeast** (refrigerate after opening)
- **Yogurt, vegan**: coconut milk or rice milk

Recommended Kitchen Tools

The following tools and appliances will come in handy when baking the recipes in this book. I don't expect you to go out and buy all of them, but if you plan to get serious about your baking, you may want to start collecting various items over the next few years. Many of these tools you probably already have in your kitchen if you cook or bake, as they are basics. For those of you for whom these items are new, please know that you can generally make do with the bare basics. The most important items, the "must-haves," are those that you use for measuring, because measurements must be exact to ensure proper results. Pan size is equally important. Even a 1-inch difference can change the results of your final product. Otherwise, you can improvise with your tools. If you don't have a rolling pin handy, you can use a wine bottle on its side. If you don't have a biscuit cutter, use an upside-down juice glass. And although I tested most of my recipes using an electric stand mixer, you can whip these up the good old-fashioned way, by using a mixing bowl and a wooden spoon—just work a little harder, and throw in some elbow grease.

SMALL KITCHEN APPLIANCES

Coffee grinder or mini-chop—For making homemade flaxseed meal (see Resources, page 177).

Electric stand mixer—A stand mixer is a multipurpose workhorse that may well become the love of your life. Mine is turquoise, and makes me smile daily.

Food processor, with multiple blades—In addition to making crumb toppings and sometimes dough in my food processor, I also use it for shredding carrots and apples, which is the quickest method.

Handheld electric mixer—Use anywhere a recipe calls for a stand mixer, following the visual cues as written; the timing may differ very slightly, but the end results will be the same.

Microwave oven—A microwave oven will simplify melting chocolate, gently softening vegetable shortening, and lightly warming liquids.

MEASURING TOOLS

Dry measuring cups, preferably metal—For measuring solid and semisolid ingredients (such as vegetable shortening and SunButter), which allows you to level ingredients with a straightedge.

Liquid measuring cups, preferably glass—These allow you to read measurements from the side, and have a spout for pouring.

Measuring spoons—If you do a lot of baking, you may wish to purchase two sets. And to make life easier,

try to find a set that includes a 1½-tablespoon measuring spoon; also look for a 2-tablespoon scoop.

KNIVES

Chopping knife (8-inch or 9-inch chef's knife)—For chopping and cutting.

Paring knives—For peeling and slicing fruit and vegetables.

Serrated knife—A long serrated knife is essential for evening the tops of layer cakes, slicing bread, and cutting up baking chocolate.

Slicing knives (long, thin blade)—For cutting things like . . . cake!

BAKING TOOLS

Apple corer—Removes core and cuts apples into eight even pieces. This tool is indispensable when making apple pie. It's a huge time-saver.

Biscuit cutters—For making biscuits or perfectly round, rolled cookies.

Cake stand—A cake stand is certainly not essential, but it really lends a flourish to your presentation and makes frosting a cake simpler.

Citrus juicer or reamer—I use lemon juice and lime juice all the time in my baking and cooking. A juicer or reamer will help squeeze out every last drop of juice from your citrus.

Cookie press—For making pressed cookies, such as Orange Spritz Cookies (page 65), in a vast array of shapes. See Resources, page 177, for shopping information.

Decorative cutters—For cutting small shapes for decorating pie crusts, etc.

Flexible heatproof spatula—As essential as wooden spoons. You will use your flexible heatproof spatula until you wear it out. Look for silicone spatulas. They are great for mixing, folding in ingredients, scraping down the sides of a bowl while mixing, and transferring every last drop of batter or dough from your bowl to the pan.

Frosting spatula or offset spatula—A multipurpose tool, and essential to creating that coveted swirl when frosting cakes and cupcakes.

Instant-read thermometer—For checking the temperature while dough is rising, testing the internal temperature of baked goods in seconds, and more.

Kitchen timer—Although most modern ovens have a built-in timer, you will sometimes have to keep track of two items at once, so it's a good idea to have a second timer.

Mechanical pastry bag—Makes frosting and icing baked goods fun and easy (not to mention no-fuss cleanup!).

Metal spatula—A wide, thin-edged spatula that helps easily transfer hot baked goods from pans to cooling racks.

Microplane (also called a rasp grater or zester)—A stainless steel grater with tiny, razor-sharp teeth that is worth its weight in gold. It's the penultimate for zesting citrus and is also perfect for grating chocolate, nutmeg, and ginger.

Mixing bowls—Every kitchen should have a set of mixing bowls, from large to small. Preferably, they should be glass or ceramic, and microwave safe.

Muffin liners—Muffin liners make for easy removal from the muffin pan and easy cleanup, keep your muffins and cupcakes from drying out too quickly, and are often decorative as well. I always bake my muffins and cupcakes in liners, even if I'm using a nonstick pan, for all of these reasons. If you choose to bake without them (to save trees, because you're out of them, or personal preference), be sure to grease the muffin pan.

Oven thermometer—Keeping the proper temperature is key to successful results. Being off by more than 5 or 10 degrees will greatly alter your final results. Do not depend on your oven's own thermometer: go out and buy yourself an additional one.

Parchment paper—For lining baking sheets, rolling out crusts, etc. (I have used many brands, and find Whole Foods 365 Natural Parchment Paper the easiest to work with, and it's cheap!)

Pastry blender—A sturdy metal tool that works shortening into your dry ingredients for crusts, biscuits, crumbles, etc.

Pastry brushes, small, medium, and large—Most bakers recommend using brushes with tightly woven natural bristles, but I also use the silicone bristle brush from Le Creuset, because I find it is easier to clean.

Pastry cutter—Used to cut lattice strips for pie crusts, or to cut out rolled cookies or crackers. Look for one with a fluted edge for the prettiest results.

Rolling pin—I've been using the same rolling pin since high school. I find that the heavier ones work better. They have heft behind them to roll more evenly. I bought myself a more expensive tapered dowel, but it's too light and rolls unevenly, making the person do all the work, instead of rolling like a rolling pin should!

Ruler—For measuring pans, etc.

Shaped cookie cutters—For making rolled cookies.

Sieve—A sieve can be used to sift dry ingredients, just like a sifter, or to finely strain liquids to extract pulp and/or seeds.

Sifter—I recommend sifting for lighter baked goods such as cupcakes. Sifters are great for sifting in dry ingredients such as flour, confectioners' sugar, and cocoa powder.

Silicone spatula—A sturdy silicone spatula will help you transfer items while protecting surfaces from being scratched.

Toothpicks—For checking doneness on smaller baked goods.

Vegetable peeler—For peeling apples, potatoes, carrots, etc.

Whisks, metal and nonstick—It's good to have whisks of varying sizes. I use a large metal whisk to combine dry ingredients, a small metal whisk to combine egg replacer with rice milk, and a medium-sized nonstick whisk to whisk things such as pastry custard, pudding, and sauces while they're heating, so as not to scratch the pan.

Wire cooling rack—A cooling rack is necessary to cool baked goods evenly by allowing air to circulate so they don't steam themselves from the bottom.

Wooden board—A large wooden board is great for rolling out dough if you don't have a built-in wooden surface elsewhere (I don't).

Wooden skewers—For checking doneness of cakes, etc.

Wooden spoons—Good wooden spoons will last you a lifetime. You should have a couple for stirring any pot, bowl, or dish that you don't want scratched.

MISCELLANEOUS KITCHEN TOOLS

Colander—For straining and washing fruits and vegetables.

Cutting boards, wooden and plastic—I prefer to have one cutting board that's designated as the "onions, garlic, and other strong savories" board, because I have found that certain fruits will pick up strong flavors if chopped on the same board. For example, pineapple has the uncanny knack of picking up any trace of garlic, no matter how long ago it was chopped on that board.

Dish cloths, tea towels, cloth napkins—I use dish cloths, tea towels, and cloth napkins to cover yeasted baked goods while they are rising and to dry freshly washed fruit and veggies, in addition to their normal uses.

Kitchen shears—For shearing, of course.

Oven mitts and pot holders—Unless you are my great-grandmother Dora, who supposedly spent so much time at the oven she could transfer baked goods with her bare hands, you'll want to protect your precious digits from getting burned with oven mitts and pot holders. Invest in good ones, or else you may still get burned through the flimsy cloth.

Plastic wrap—A kitchen necessity, for tightly wrapping bowls, containers, or wrapping up dough to chill.

POTS AND PANS

Cast-iron skillet, 10-inch—A well-seasoned cast-iron skillet is the way they did nonstick in the old days. And quite frankly, it's still the way I prefer. You can use this pan for cooking on the stove top as well as for baking. Cooking in a cast-iron skillet adds iron to your diet. Just don't cook with acidic ingredients such as lemon juice, tomatoes, or vinegar in your cast-iron skillet or you'll wind up destroying the pan and getting a horrible, bitter flavor.

Heavy saucepans, with lids—Every kitchen needs a few saucepans, if only to boil water!

BAKING PANS AND BAKING DISHES

Baking sheets (also called cookie sheets)—I recommend using heavy-duty aluminum baking sheets. Dark metal sheets, such as nonstick sheets, will brown the baked goods more quickly, so if using these, you may need to reduce the temperature by 25 degrees or shorten your baking time.

Bundt pan or tube pan, 10-inch—A nonstick Bundt pan or tube pan is great to have on hand for whipping up no-fuss cakes. They come in a variety of pretty designs.

Cornstick pan—Most old-fashioned cornstick pans make seven cornsticks at a time. Look for heavy cast-iron pans. They need to be well seasoned to allow for the cornsticks to flip out easily. You can buy new pans or comb yard sales and thrift shops for a pan with a little history.

Loaf pan—I use a standard 9 by 5-inch loaf pan for the recipes in this book.

Madeleine pan—Only essential if you wish to make madeleines, which I recommend, because they are tasty little sponge cakes that are great for breakfast, teatime, or dessert.

Muffin pans—One or two standard twelve-count muffin pans will allow you to make muffins and cupcakes galore.

Nonstick tart pan with removable bottom, 9½-inch—The removable bottom is a great modern invention, allowing you to produce perfect, professional-looking tarts time and time again.

Pie dish, 9-inch—Invest in a good-quality ceramic pie dish; it will serve you well for many years to come. You may also use a glass pie dish for these recipes.

Rectangular baking dishes, ceramic or glass—I mostly use an 11 by 7-inch dish.

Round cake pans (two), 8-inch and 9-inch, heavy-duty aluminum—All the layer cake recipes in this book call for 8-inch pans, but it's a good idea to have a set of both.

Square baking pans/dishes, 8-inch and 9-inch, ceramic, glass, or heavy-duty aluminum—I like to bake fruited desserts such as crumbles and crisps in ceramic or glass, but use heavy-duty aluminum for baking brownies and cakes. Please note that darker pans will cause baked goods to cook more quickly.

2

How to Bake *Allergen-Free*

So, what are we working with? And what are we working without? Well, for starters, we're working without wheat and other gluten-containing flours, eggs, dairy, soy, and nuts. "But aren't those the staples of baked goods?" you might ask. Maybe in the old days, but there's a new cake in town! It's vegan, tastes great, is good for you, and kicks allergenic ingredients to the curb. So what *are* we working with, then? The possibilities are endless. Follow me, as I lead you through swapping out the allergens.

Replacing Eggs

Eggs provide moisture, richness, binding, and leavening. I use a variety of alternative ingredients in place of eggs.

APPLESAUCE

Applesauce works as a binding agent and is also a great substitute for eggs or oil or shortening when you want to reduce the fat.

1/4 cup unsweetened applesauce = 1 egg

BAKING SODA AND VINEGAR

This is an old baking trick from World War II days, when eggs were rationed. It provides leavening in place of eggs. Add the baking soda to the dry ingredients and add the vinegar to the liquid. Wait to combine the dry and liquid ingredients until the very last minute, because the chemical reaction occurs as soon as the baking soda and vinegar meet, and you must get your goodie straight into the oven!

1 teaspoon baking soda + 1 teaspoon cider vinegar (or distilled white vinegar) = 1 egg

BANANA

Works similarly to applesauce, but has a much more distinct flavor. I only use it when I want to taste banana.

1/2 banana, mashed = 1 egg

EGG REPLACER

Egg replacer is great for leavening and binding. I use Ener-G egg replacer because it is manufactured in a facility free of all common allergens. Egg replacer works best when whisked together with a liquid, using a small whisk. Be sure to beat it until slightly frothy and all the lumps have dissolved before adding it to a recipe.

1 1/2 teaspoons Ener-G egg replacer mixed with 2 tablespoons rice milk or water = 1 egg

FLAXSEED MEAL

I love the effect of "flax eggs"; it works just like an egg, doing everything but leavening. It's moist, rich, and binding. However, I have used flax eggs sparingly in this book, because it is difficult to find totally "clean" flax. It's often processed in facilities along with tree nuts or other allergens. So be sure to check with the manufacturer before consuming flax if cross-contamination is a concern for you. See Resources, page 177, for brands that are manufactured in a peanut-free, tree nut–free facility.

1 tablespoon flaxseed meal mixed with 3 tablespoons warm water = 1 egg

PRUNE PURÉE (AKA BABY FOOD!)

Again, works similarly to applesauce, with a sweeter flavor.

4 1/2- to 5-ounce jar prune purée = 1 egg

VEGAN YOGURT

Vegan yogurt is great for adding moisture and binding. I use it in place of eggs, but also in place of buttermilk or cream. I use coconut milk yogurt (see page 178) and rice milk yogurt in these recipes. I prefer coconut milk yogurt, but please note that the allergy world is on the fence about coconut. Most people with tree nut allergies are *not* allergic to coconut, and it's an extremely rare allergy, but still, check with your allergist before consuming it.

If coconut milk is not an option for you, use rice milk yogurt instead.

> 1/4 cup vegan yogurt = 1 egg

Replacing Dairy

In baking, dairy is primarily used to provide moisture but also contributes to flavor and body, and its sugars help with browning. Buttermilk is often used to create a very tender crumb, and cream is valued for its richness and feel of creaminess. Butter is used in a multitude of ways, lending a warm, sweet richness to baked goods. Vegan milks and yogurts can easily mimic all of these qualities, with a little ingenuity.

COW'S MILK

Replacing cow's milk is pretty much a no-brainer because even our local supermarkets now sell soymilk and rice milk. Because this book also eliminates soy, I use rice milk anywhere you might traditionally use cow's milk. I have chosen rice milk because it is easiest to find and has a mild flavor, but if you wish to substitute another nondairy milk in my recipes, please feel free to do so. I give several other dairy-free, soy-free, gluten-free, and nut-free options below.

> 1 cup nondairy milk = 1 cup cow's milk

Coconut Milk

Coconut is very rich. It can be used in baking, but bear in mind that it is thick and sweet. (Again, the allergy world is on the fence about coconut. Most say it's a member of the date family, a few say it's a tree nut. Most people with tree nut allergies are not allergic to coconut, and it's an extremely rare allergy, but still, check with your allergist before consuming it.)

Hemp Milk

Hemp milk is the most nutritious of nondairy milks, and it has a rich, nutty flavor. Look for it at Whole Foods or your local health food store. See Resources, page 177, for gluten-free, nut-free hemp milk brands.

Rice Milk

Rice milk is generally made from brown rice. It is a little thinner than other nondairy milks, but it still provides yummy moistness. Rice milk is commercially available just about everywhere. See Resources, page 177, for a list of gluten-free rice milk brands.

BUTTERMILK

You can easily make your own nondairy buttermilk at home. To make 1 cup of buttermilk, add 1 tablespoon lemon juice or cider vinegar to 1 cup nondairy milk, and let stand for about 10 minutes to sour.

YOGURT, CREAM, AND SOUR CREAM

I use coconut milk yogurt and rice milk yogurt in place of yogurt, cream, and sour cream. I prefer coconut milk yogurt because it has a better texture and the tang of traditional dairy yogurt. If coconut milk is not an option for you, use rice milk yogurt instead. And if you can eat soy, then by all means, substitute soy yogurt.

BUTTER

Ah, butter . . . the backbone of Western baking. Or is it? I've been delighted to find you can still make awesome "buttery" baked goods *without* butter. Here are my favorite substitutes for old-fashioned butter.

Canola Oil

I generally use canola oil in my recipes because it's easy to find, healthful, and mild. See Resources, page 177, for brands that are manufactured in a peanut-free, tree nut–free facility. Alternatively, you can use rice bran oil, another light, healthful oil (again, check Resources, page 177, for "safe" brands). If you choose to use another type of vegetable oil, pick one that you know is safe for you and that has a mild flavor. I like safflower oil and sunflower oil, or you may choose to bake with extra-light olive oil.

$\frac{1}{3}$ cup canola oil = $\frac{1}{2}$ cup butter

Dairy-Free, Soy-Free Vegetable Shortening

Organic, nonhydrogenated, cholesterol-free, this shortening bakes up nice and light. See Resources, page 177, for brands that are manufactured in a peanut-free, tree nut–free facility. If the shortening is too solid to measure out easily, warm it in the microwave for about 15 seconds to soften it slightly. If it is too soft and soupy because it's a very warm day, chill the shortening in the refrigerator for 30 minutes, or until firmer. Also, be sure to pack and pack again when measuring, because it has a tendency to create air pockets. Really push it down into the measuring cup to make sure you're getting an exact measure.

1 cup dairy-free, soy-free vegetable shortening = 1 cup unsalted butter

Replacing Nuts and Nut Butters

The past few years have seen the advent of Sun-Butter. SunButter (aka sunflower seed butter) is a great replacement for peanut butter and other nut butters. It is available at Trader Joe's, Whole Foods, and many local health food stores. It's also popping up on some supermarket shelves. There is a small chance that containers of SunButter could be cross-contaminated with soy, which is also processed at that facility. To be extra careful, you can make your own sunflower seed butter using peanut-free sunflower seeds that you know to be safe. You can now buy "safe" sunflower seeds for snacking, or to use in baking, though you may have to order these online. See Resources, page 177, for peanut-free, tree nut–free brands.

Replacing Wheat Flour and Other Gluten Flours

This is perhaps the trickiest part of baking allergen-free. It's not so hard to bake gluten-free if you can still use eggs, butter, and nut flours, but figuring out how to bake without *any* of them has been a learning curve for me. But I persevered and am happy to report that I've come out triumphant. Baking allergen-free and gluten-free is not only possible, but it's also downright delicious!

GLUTEN-FREE, ALLERGEN-FREE FLOURS

Here's what you have to choose from: rice, corn, potato, tapioca, bean, garfava, sorghum, quinoa, millet, buckwheat, arrowroot, amaranth, teff, montina, and flax flours.

Whoa, that's a lot of flours! And trickier still, most of them can't be used on their own—they must be mixed like you're doing AP chemistry. They can't be swapped out cup for cup for wheat flour, and they require varying amounts of xanthan gum from recipe to recipe. So to make things simple for *you*, I've created a Basic Gluten-Free Flour Mix that you can whip up and store in your fridge.

Basic Gluten-Free Flour Mix

MAKES 6 CUPS

The key to the very best gluten-free baked goods is Authentic Foods superfine brown rice flour; it is the Cadillac, or cashmere, of brown rice flours and is worth its weight in gold. It is not grainy like other rice flours, and bakes the most fantastic cookies, cakes, pie crusts, and so on. If you can't find it at your local natural foods market or Whole Foods, order it online. Both Ener-G and Bob's Red Mill brown rice flours will also work in these recipes, but they won't turn out quite as well. I do not recommend Arrowhead Mills brown rice flour, which I find too gritty. The brands of potato starch and tapioca flour or starch are not important; I find them all inter-changeable. (Please see Resources, page 177, for more information.)

4 cups superfine brown rice flour
1 1/3 cups potato starch (*not* potato flour)
2/3 cup tapioca flour (also called tapioca starch)

1. To measure flour, use a large spoon to scoop flour into the measuring cup, then level it off with the back of a knife or straightedge. Do *not* use the measuring cup itself to scoop your flour when measuring! It will compact the flour and you will wind up with too much for the recipe.

2. Combine all ingredients in a gallon-size zipper-top bag. Shake until well blended. Store in the refrigerator until ready to use.

Important Tips for Successful Baking

1. Please read all recipes through at least once before making them.
2. Measure out all your ingredients before you start.
3. Make sure your oven is properly calibrated and keeps a correct temperature.
4. Invest in a good digital timer, so cooking times are exact.
5. Use heavy baking sheets and quality pans, so the bottoms of your goodies don't burn.
6. Most of all, do not substitute ingredients! These recipes are carefully written to provide good results with gluten-free flours and allergen-free ingredients. Substituting alternate ingredients can throw the whole recipe out of balance.
7. Use nesting measuring cups for solids and glass measuring cups for liquids.
8. To measure flour, use a large spoon to scoop flour into the measuring cup, then level it off with the back of a knife. Do *not* use the measuring cup itself to scoop your flour when measuring! It will compact the flour and you will wind up with too much for the recipe.
9. Check the level of liquid ingredients at eye level from the side.
10. Always pack brown sugar. White sugar, confectioners' sugar, date sugar, and maple sugar may be scooped with a measuring cup or spooned into the measuring cup.
11. Measure fruit purées as solids in nesting cups, for an exact measure.

A FEW WORDS ABOUT MY CHOICE OF FLOURS

Almost all recipes in this book are made with a blend of superfine brown rice flour, potato starch, and tapioca flour. I have chosen these flours/starches not only because they are great for gluten-free baking, but also because they are generally the easiest gluten-free flours for the general public to find. But most important, I have chosen these three flours/starches because they carry the least risk of cross-contamination. Most gluten-free flours are still being processed in the same facilities as tree nut flours (such as almond flour) and other common allergens. If the risk of cross-contamination is an issue for you, you can purchase all three of these flours from Ener-G, risk-free.

For the Gluten-Free Bread Flour Mix (page 158), I use "sweet" sorghum flour and millet flour mixed with tapioca flour and potato starch. Larger manufacturers of sorghum flour, such as Bob's Red Mill and Authentic Foods, use facilities that produce tree nut flours. If potential cross-contamination with tree nuts poses a risk for you, look for smaller grain producers that often produce only that one flour. You can order online and have the flour shipped to you. I provide product recommendations in the Resources section.

A number of recipes include some "old-world" gluten-free flours now available on the market, such as quinoa flour, corn flour, amaranth flour, and buckwheat flour. I also use gluten-free oats in several recipes, which luckily have hit the market in the past year or so. If you have concerns or questions about the manufacturing practices of these products, please contact the company directly.

Orange Scones (page 35), Glazed Vanilla Scones (page 36), and Cherry Oat Scones (page 37)

3

MUFFINS, SCONES, *Biscuits*, *Quick Breads*, AND COFFEE CAKES

love breakfast. I wake up famished and so do my sons. And there is no better way to roll out of bed than with the lure of a high-fiber, energy-packed tasty baked treat. Muffins, scones, biscuits, quick breads, and coffee cakes are all easy to make and quick to bake, making breakfast the perfect time to start your journey into allergen-free baking. These wholesome goodies are a great way to introduce your family and friends to nutrient-dense, gluten-free flours like millet, buckwheat, and quinoa by combining them with fruits, calcium-enriched rice milk, and/or protein-rich seeds for a power-packed slam dunk to begin your day.

Whether it's weekday breakfast or a weekend brunch, you can turn your kitchen into your own personal bakery with these quick, wholesome, tummy-tempting treats. Most of these recipes are also easy enough to be baked with kids. And most important, these recipes are forgiving, so if this is your first foray into the world of egg replacer, xanthan gum, and baking with fruit purées, they'll ease you in gently. You'll see how simple it really is, and quickly find yourself effortlessly turning out your own specialty goods on a daily basis. And if you don't feel like making them on a daily basis, you're in luck, because these beauties freeze well, and generally keep for several days, covered, at room temperature. So let's get baking.

Morning Glory Muffins

MAKES 12 MUFFINS

These muffins are scrumptious and chock-full of beta-carotene, phytonutrients, protein, and fiber, with no refined sugar. What better way to start your day than with a Morning Glory Muffin?

1/2 cup canola oil

1 cup light agave nectar

1 tablespoon pure vanilla extract

2 teaspoons ground cinnamon

2 cups grated/shredded carrots (I use my food processor for this)

1 large apple, peeled, cored, and grated/shredded

1 tablespoon freshly squeezed lemon juice

1 cup raisins

1/2 cup sunflower seeds (raw or roasted)

3 cups Basic Gluten-Free Flour Mix (page 19)

3/4 teaspoon xanthan gum

11/2 teaspoons baking soda

1/2 teaspoon salt

1. Preheat the oven to 350°F. Line a muffin pan with 12 muffin liners.

2. In the bowl of a stand mixer fitted with the paddle attachment, combine the canola oil and agave nectar. Mix on medium speed for about 20 seconds.

3. Add the vanilla and cinnamon and mix for 20 seconds.

4. In a separate bowl, combine the shredded carrots and shredded apple, and then toss with the lemon juice. Add to the mixing bowl. Mix for about 20 seconds.

5. Mix in the raisins and sunflower seeds.

6. In a separate bowl, combine the flour mix, xanthan gum, baking soda, and salt.

7. Add the dry ingredients to the wet and mix until just combined.

8. Fill the liners to the rim with batter.

9. Bake in the center of the oven for 35 minutes, or until lovely golden brown on top, rotating the pan halfway through. Let cool in the pan for 5 minutes before transferring to a cooling rack.

Tip ■ If using salted sunflower seeds, reduce the salt to 1/4 teaspoon. To buy sunflower seeds that are processed in a dedicated peanut-free facility, go to www.peanutfreeplanet.com. See Resources, page 177.

Banana Flax Muffins

MAKES 12 MUFFINS

These hearty muffins are tasty and energy packed. I find they're a particular favorite with the toddler set.

1/4 cup canola oil
1 cup light agave nectar
1 1/2 cups mashed ripe banana
2 tablespoons freshly squeezed lemon juice
1 1/2 teaspoons ground cinnamon
1/4 teaspoon ground nutmeg
3/4 cup golden flaxseed meal

2 1/2 cups Basic Gluten-Free Flour Mix
   (page 19)
3/4 teaspoon xanthan gum
1 1/2 teaspoons baking soda
1/2 teaspoon salt
1 cup raisins

1. Preheat the oven to 350°F. Line a muffin pan with 12 muffin liners.

2. In the bowl of a stand mixer fitted with the paddle attachment, combine the canola oil and agave nectar, mixing on medium speed for about 20 seconds.

3. Add the mashed banana, lemon juice, cinnamon, and nutmeg, and mix for 20 seconds. Add the flax meal and mix until combined, about 10 seconds.

4. In a separate bowl, combine the flour mix, xanthan gum, baking soda, and salt.

5. Add the dry ingredients to the wet and mix on low until just combined, about 20 seconds.

6. Turn off the mixer and fold in the raisins.

7. Fill the liners to the rim with batter. They will be heaping.

8. Bake in the center of the oven for 25 minutes, or until lovely golden brown on top, rotating the pan halfway through. Transfer the muffins to a cooling rack.

Gingerbread Muffins

MAKES 12 MUFFINS

Gingerbread muffins are perfect for a decadent holiday breakfast or a healthy snack all year round. These muffins get extremely hot during baking, so it's best to let some of the steam escape before eating them. They're moist, like banana bread or cake, and are best once they've cooled and set a bit. (You don't have to wait, but they do reach peak yumminess after resting for 30 minutes.)

1/2 cup canola oil

1 cup plus 2 tablespoons light agave nectar

1 1/2 cups unsweetened applesauce

1 tablespoon ground ginger

3 cups Basic Gluten-Free Flour Mix (page 19)

3/4 teaspoon xanthan gum

1 1/2 teaspoons baking soda

1/2 teaspoon salt

1 cup plus 2 tablespoons raisins or currants

1. Preheat the oven to 350°F. Line a muffin pan with 12 muffin liners.

2. In the bowl of a stand mixer fitted with the paddle attachment, combine the canola oil and agave nectar, mixing on medium speed for about 20 seconds.

3. Add the applesauce and ginger and mix for about 20 seconds.

4. In a separate bowl, combine the flour mix, xanthan gum, baking soda, and salt.

5. Add the dry ingredients to the wet and mix until just combined.

6. Turn off the mixer and fold in the raisins.

7. Fill the liners to the rim with batter.

8. Bake in the center of the oven for 40 minutes, or until lovely golden brown on top, rotating the pan halfway through. Let cool in the pan for 5 minutes before transferring to a cooling rack. Let cool for at least 30 minutes before eating.

Plum Coffee Cake Muffins

MAKES 12 MUFFINS

These taste fancy but are very easy to make. Perfect for a weekend brunch! I like making them in early summer during plum season. They are delicate and pretty.

Topping

1/2 cup firmly packed brown sugar

1/4 cup Basic Gluten-Free Flour Mix (page 19)

1 teaspoon ground cinnamon

Pinch of salt

1/4 cup dairy-free, soy-free vegetable shortening, at room temperature

Muffins

1/2 cup canola oil

3/4 cup light agave nectar

2 teaspoons pure vanilla extract

1 teaspoon ground cinnamon

1/2 teaspoon allspice

1 1/2 cups unsweetened applesauce

3 cups Basic Gluten-Free Flour Mix (page 19)

3/4 teaspoon xanthan gum

1 1/2 teaspoons baking soda

1/2 teaspoon salt

1 cup diced plums (they should be ripe, but still firm enough to cube into centimeter-sized chunks)

1. Preheat the oven to 350°F. Line a muffin pan with 12 muffin liners.

2. To make the topping, combine the brown sugar, flour mix, cinnamon, and salt, using a fork. Add the shortening, and use the fork to work it in until it forms a crumbly texture. Set aside.

3. To make the muffins, in the bowl of a stand mixer fitted with the paddle attachment, combine the canola oil and agave nectar. Mix on medium speed for about 20 seconds. Add the vanilla, cinnamon, and allspice. Mix in the applesauce.

4. In a separate bowl, combine the flour mix, xanthan gum, baking soda, and salt.

5. Add the dry ingredients to the wet and mix until just combined.

6. Fold in the diced plums.

7. Divide the batter evenly among the liners. These muffins will be heaping. Sprinkle the muffins with the crumb topping, pressing it into the batter lightly with your fingers.

8. Bake in the center of the oven for 35 minutes, or until the crumb topping is golden brown, rotating the pan halfway through. Remove from the oven and let cool for about 5 minutes before gently transferring the muffins to a cooling rack.

Tip ■ These muffins are also great made with Apriums or Pluots, hybrid fruits that are part plum, part apricot.

Blackberry Quinoa Muffins (page 33)
and Orange Cranberry Muffins (opposite)

Orange Cranberry Muffins

MAKES 12 MUFFINS

Orange and cranberries are a perfect pairing. Transport yourself to a New England bed and breakfast with these sweet and tart little gems.

2 cups granulated sugar, plus 2 teaspoons for sprinkling (optional)

1 tablespoon Ener-G egg replacer mixed with 1/4 cup rice milk

1 cup orange juice

2 teaspoons orange zest

3 tablespoons canola oil

3 cups Basic Gluten-Free Flour Mix (page 19)

3/4 teaspoon xanthan gum

4 teaspoons double-acting baking powder

1/2 teaspoon salt

1 teaspoon ground cinnamon

1 1/2 cups fresh or frozen cranberries

1. Preheat the oven to 350°F. Line a muffin pan with 12 muffin liners.

2. In the bowl of a stand mixer fitted with the paddle attachment, combine 2 cups of the sugar and the egg replacer, mixing on medium speed for about 30 seconds.

3. Add the orange juice, orange zest, and canola oil. Mix for about 30 seconds.

4. In a separate bowl, whisk together the flour mix, xanthan gum, baking powder, salt, and cinnamon.

5. Add the dry ingredients to the wet and mix until just combined, about 30 seconds, scraping down the sides of the bowl as necessary.

6. Turn off the mixer and fold in the cranberries.

7. Fill the liners to the rim with batter. Sprinkle the tops of the muffins with the remaining 2 teaspoons of sugar.

8. Bake in the center of the oven 35 to 40 minutes, rotating the pan halfway through. Bake until lovely golden brown on top and a skewer inserted into the center of a muffin comes out clean. Let cool in the pan for 5 minutes before transferring to a cooling rack. You may need to gently run a butter knife under the edges of the muffin tops to loosen them slightly.

Blueberry Millet Muffins

MAKES 12 MUFFINS

Millet adds nice texture to this traditional favorite. Blueberry muffins are always a crowd-pleaser. Bake up a big batch, store them in the freezer, and you'll always have breakfast on hand.

1 cup rice milk

1 tablespoon freshly squeezed lemon juice

1 cup granulated sugar, plus 2 teaspoons for sprinkling (optional)

1 tablespoon Ener-G egg replacer mixed with 1/4 cup rice milk

2 teaspoons pure vanilla extract

1/4 cup canola oil

1 teaspoon lemon zest

2 cups Basic Gluten-Free Flour Mix (page 19)

1 cup millet flour

3/4 teaspoon xanthan gum

4 teaspoons double-acting baking powder

1/2 teaspoon salt

1 1/2 cups fresh or frozen blueberries

1/3 cup blueberry jam (preferably fruit-only)

1. Preheat the oven to 350°F. Line a muffin pan with 12 muffin liners.

2. In a small bowl, combine the rice milk and lemon juice and set aside.

3. In the bowl of a stand mixer fitted with the paddle attachment, combine 1 cup of the sugar and the egg replacer, mixing on medium speed for about 20 seconds.

4. Add the rice milk mixture, vanilla, canola oil, and lemon zest. Mix for 30 seconds.

5. In a separate bowl, combine the flour mix, millet flour, xanthan gum, baking powder, and salt.

6. Add the dry ingredients to the wet and mix until just combined, about 20 seconds.

7. Turn off the mixer and fold in the blueberries.

8. Fill the liners to the rim with batter. Spoon 1 teaspoon of blueberry jam onto the top of each muffin, pushing it into the center slightly. Use a chopstick or skewer to swirl the jam into the muffins. Sprinkle the tops of the muffins with the remaining 2 teaspoons sugar.

9. Bake in the center of the oven for 30 to 35 minutes, or until a lovely golden on top, rotating the pan halfway through. Transfer the muffins to a cooling rack.

Apricot Cornmeal Muffins

MAKES 12 MUFFINS

My son Monte and I both love fresh apricots. Living in Southern California, we're lucky to get them in abundance. I created this recipe for him. He loves the subtly sweet cornmeal muffin punctuated by bites of tart apricot. (Okay, I admit I'm paraphrasing—he is only five.)

1 cup vanilla vegan yogurt

2/3 cup rice milk

1 tablespoon freshly squeezed lemon juice

1 cup granulated sugar, plus 2 teaspoons for sprinkling

1/2 cup dairy-free, soy-free vegetable shortening

1 tablespoon Ener-G egg replacer mixed with 1/4 cup rice milk

2 teaspoons pure vanilla extract

2 1/4 cups Basic Gluten-Free Flour Mix (page 19)

3/4 cup fine cornmeal

3/4 teaspoon xanthan gum

1 1/2 teaspoons double-acting baking powder

1 1/2 teaspoons baking soda

1/2 teaspoon salt

1 cup diced apricots (they should be ripe, but still firm enough to cube into centimeter-sized chunks)

1. Preheat the oven to 350°F. Line a muffin pan with 12 muffin liners.

2. In a bowl, combine the yogurt, rice milk, and lemon juice and set aside.

3. In the bowl of a stand mixer fitted with the paddle attachment, combine 1 cup of the sugar, the shortening, and the egg replacer, mixing on medium speed for 20 seconds.

4. Add the rice milk mixture and the vanilla. Mix for 20 seconds.

5. In a separate bowl, combine the flour mix, cornmeal, xanthan gum, baking powder, baking soda, and salt.

6. Add the dry ingredients to the wet and mix on low speed until just combined, about 20 seconds.

7. Turn off the mixer and fold in the apricots.

8. Fill the liners with batter. They will be heaping. Smooth the tops slightly with a knife. Sprinkle the tops of the muffins with the remaining 2 teaspoons sugar.

9. Bake in the center of the oven for 30 minutes, or until lovely golden brown on top, rotating once about halfway through. Transfer the muffins to a cooling rack.

Buckwheat Apple Muffins

MAKES 12 MUFFINS

Buckwheat is such a great old-world flour. Its distinctive, slightly sweet, earthy flavor pairs extremely well with tart apple.

1/2 cup canola oil
1 cup light agave nectar
1 1/2 cups unsweetened applesauce
1 teaspoon pure vanilla extract
1 teaspoon ground cinnamon
3 cups buckwheat flour

3/4 teaspoon xanthan gum
1 1/2 teaspoons baking soda
1/2 teaspoon salt
1 large Granny Smith apple, peeled and diced
   (about 1 1/2 cups)

1. Preheat the oven to 350°F. Line a muffin pan with 12 muffin liners.

2. In the bowl of a stand mixer fitted with the paddle attachment, combine the canola oil and agave nectar, mixing on medium speed for about 20 seconds.

3. Add the applesauce, vanilla, and cinnamon. Mix for about 20 seconds.

4. In a separate bowl, combine the buckwheat flour, xanthan gum, baking soda, and salt.

5. Add the dry ingredients to the wet and mix until just combined, about 20 seconds.

6. Fold in the apple.

7. Fill the liners to the rim with batter. These muffins will be heaping, and the batter will be thick.

8. Bake in the center of the oven for 25 minutes, or until lovely golden brown on top, rotating the pan halfway through. Let cool in the pan for 5 minutes before transferring to a cooling rack.

Blackberry Quinoa Muffins

MAKES 12 LARGE MUFFINS

These tasty, not-too-sweet muffins are packed with protein-rich quinoa and plenty of antioxidant-rich fruit. Add a glass of calcium-enriched OJ or rice milk, and you have a complete breakfast.

2¼ cups quinoa flour

¾ cup corn flour

¾ teaspoon xanthan gum

2 teaspoons baking soda

½ teaspoon salt

½ cup canola oil

¾ cup light agave nectar

2 teaspoons pure vanilla extract

1½ cups unsweetened applesauce

2 teaspoons cider vinegar

2 cups fresh or frozen blackberries (frozen are easier to work with), lightly tossed with a little corn flour, quinoa flour, or Basic Gluten-Free Flour Mix

1. Preheat the oven to 350°F. Line a muffin pan with 12 muffin liners.

2. Whisk together the quinoa flour, corn flour, xanthan gum, baking soda, and salt. Set aside.

3. In the bowl of a stand mixer fitted with the paddle attachment, combine the canola oil and agave nectar, mixing on medium speed for about 20 seconds. Add the vanilla and applesauce. Mix for about 20 seconds. Add the vinegar, then immediately stir in the flour mixture. Gently fold in the blackberries.

4. Divide the batter evenly among the muffin cups. Gently swirl the top of the batter with the back of a teaspoon or frosting spatula.

5. Bake in the center of the oven for 35 minutes, rotating the pan halfway through. Bake until deeply golden and a skewer inserted into the center of a muffin comes out clean. Transfer the muffins to a cooling rack.

Tip ■ Corn flour has a much finer grain than cornmeal. Look for it at your local health food store or Whole Foods.

Basic Scones

MAKES 12 SCONES

This basic scone is fantastic hot from the oven with a little vegan butter and strawberry jam. This recipe is also easily adaptable. See the variations listed below.

1 (6-ounce) container plain or vanilla vegan yogurt

3/4 cup rice milk

1 tablespoon freshly squeezed lemon juice

3 cups Basic Gluten-Free Flour Mix (page 19)

3/4 teaspoon xanthan gum

1/3 cup granulated sugar

2 tablespoons double-acting baking powder

1/4 teaspoon salt

1/3 cup canola oil

1. Preheat the oven to 400°F. Line a baking sheet with parchment paper.

2. Whisk together the yogurt, rice milk, and lemon juice. Set aside.

3. In a large bowl, whisk together the flour mix, xanthan gum, sugar, baking powder, and salt.

4. Add the rice milk mixture and canola oil, and stir with a wooden spoon until combined but still clumpy.

5. Flour a work surface lightly with a little gluten-free flour mix, and turn out the dough. Lightly flour your hands. Sprinkle the dough with a little flour mix.

6. Divide the dough in half. Pat into two 6-inch disks. Cut the disks into 6 pie-shaped wedges. Place the scones on the baking sheet.

7. Bake in the center of the oven for 15 to 17 minutes, or until lightly golden. Transfer to a cooling rack. Serve warm.

Variations ■ **Berry Scones**: Gently fold in 1 cup fresh or frozen berries after combining the wet and dry ingredients. I particularly like raspberries!

Chocolate Chip Scones: Add 1 teaspoon pure vanilla extract, and fold in 3/4 cup dairy-free, soy-free chocolate chips at the end.

Currant Scones: After whisking together the dry ingredients, add 1/2 cup currants. Then proceed with the recipe as written.

Orange Scones

MAKES 12 SCONES

A wonderful addition to a weekend brunch, these scones are perfect served alongside fruit salad.

1 (6-ounce) container vanilla vegan yogurt
3/4 cup orange juice
2 teaspoons orange zest
3 cups Basic Gluten-Free Flour Mix (page 19)
3/4 teaspoon xanthan gum
1/3 cup granulated sugar

2 tablespoons double-acting baking powder
1/4 teaspoon salt
1/3 cup canola oil
2 tablespoons rice milk
Sanding sugar

1. Preheat the oven to 400°F. Line a baking sheet with parchment paper.

2. Whisk together the yogurt, orange juice, and orange zest. Set aside.

3. In a large bowl, whisk together the flour mix, xanthan gum, granulated sugar, baking powder, and salt.

4. Add the orange juice mixture and the canola oil, and stir with a wooden spoon until combined but still clumpy.

5. Flour a work surface lightly with a little gluten-free flour mix, and turn out the dough. Lightly flour your hands. Sprinkle the dough with a little flour mix.

6. Divide the dough in half. Pat into two 6-inch disks. Cut the disks into 6 pie-shaped wedges. Place the scones on the baking sheet. Brush with the rice milk, then sprinkle liberally with sanding sugar.

7. Bake in the center of the oven for 15 minutes, or until lightly golden and the sugar is sparkling. Transfer to a cooling rack. Serve warm.

Glazed Vanilla Scones

MAKES 12 SCONES

A pretty, elegant scone, these are equally delicious with or without the glaze.

1 (6-ounce) container vanilla vegan yogurt
3/4 cup rice milk
1 tablespoon freshly squeezed lemon juice
2 teaspoons pure vanilla extract
3 cups Basic Gluten-Free Flour Mix (page 19)
3/4 teaspoon xanthan gum

1/3 cup granulated sugar
2 tablespoons double-acting baking powder
1/4 teaspoon salt
1/3 cup canola oil
1 recipe Vanilla Glaze (recipe follows)

1. Preheat the oven to 400°F. Line a baking sheet with parchment paper.

2. Whisk together the yogurt, rice milk, lemon juice, and vanilla. Set aside.

3. In a large bowl, whisk together the flour mix, xanthan gum, sugar, baking powder, and salt.

4. Add the rice milk mixture and canola oil, and stir with a wooden spoon until combined but still clumpy.

5. Flour a work surface lightly with a little gluten-free flour mix, and turn out the dough. Lightly flour your hands. Sprinkle the dough with a little flour mix.

6. Divide the dough in half. Shape into two 6-inch disks. Cut the disks into 6 pie-shaped wedges. Place the scones on the baking sheet.

7. Bake in the center of the oven for 13 minutes, or until very lightly golden. Transfer to a cooling rack. Let cool, and then spoon 1 teaspoon of glaze over the top of each scone. Let set.

Vanilla Glaze

1 cup confectioners' sugar
2 tablespoons rice milk
1/2 teaspoon pure vanilla extract

Combine all the ingredients, mixing until smooth.

Tip ■ Before glazing the scones, put a sheet of waxed paper on a baking sheet, and set the scones on the sheet. Easy cleanup!

Cherry Oat Scones

MAKES 12 SCONES

These hearty scones are a perennial favorite, and now, thanks to gluten-free oats, even those on gluten-free diets can enjoy them. Feel free to swap out other dried fruits for the cherries. Dried apricots, cranberries, raisins, chopped dates, or figs are all wonderful substitutions. These are delicious with a little vegan butter!

1 cup plus 2 tablespoons rice milk
1 tablespoon cider vinegar
2 cups Basic Gluten-Free Flour Mix (page 19)
3/4 teaspoon xanthan gum
2 tablespoons double-acting baking powder
1/3 cup granulated sugar
1/4 teaspoon salt

1/4 teaspoon ground cinnamon
11/4 cups gluten-free old-fashioned oats
1/3 cup dairy-free, soy-free vegetable shortening
1/2 cup dried cherries
Sanding sugar (optional)

1. Preheat the oven to 400°F. Line a baking sheet with parchment paper.

2. Whisk together 1 cup of the rice milk and the cider vinegar. Set aside.

3. In a large bowl, whisk together the flour mix, xanthan gum, baking powder, granulated sugar, salt, and cinnamon.

4. Add the oats and toss. Add the shortening in pieces, and work in with a pastry blender or two knives until you have a pea-sized crumb.

5. Add the cherries, tossing until combined.

6. Add the rice milk mixture and stir with a wooden spoon until combined but still clumpy.

7. Flour a work surface lightly with a little gluten-free flour mix, and turn out the dough. Lightly flour your hands. Sprinkle the dough with a little flour mix.

8. Divide the dough in half. The dough will be sticky. Shape into two 6-inch disks. Cut the disks into 6 pie-shaped wedges. Transfer the scones to the baking sheet. Brush with the remaining 2 tablespoons rice milk, then sprinkle with sanding sugar.

9. Bake in the center of the oven for 17 minutes, or until lightly golden.

10. Serve warm from the oven, or let cool on a cooling rack.

Baking Powder Biscuits

MAKES 12 BISCUITS

These biscuits are amazing served warm straight out of the oven. Eat them savory or sweet.

4 cups Basic Gluten-Free Flour Mix (page 19)
1 teaspoon xanthan gum
2 tablespoons double-acting baking powder
1 teaspoon salt

1 cup dairy-free, soy-free vegetable shortening, chilled
2 cups plain or vanilla vegan yogurt
2 tablespoons rice milk

1. Preheat the oven to 400°F. Line a baking sheet with parchment paper.

2. In a large bowl, whisk together the flour mix, xanthan gum, baking powder, and salt.

3. Cut in the chilled shortening, using a pastry blender, two knives, or your fingers, until you have a pea-sized crumb. Add the yogurt and stir until just combined, making sure you incorporate the crumbs at the bottom of the bowl.

4. Flour a work surface lightly with a little gluten-free flour mix, and turn out the dough. Lightly flour your hands. Sprinkle the dough with a little flour mix.

5. Gently pat the dough into a 1-inch-thick disk, pressing in any loose bits. Do not over-handle the dough!

6. Use a 2¹/₂-inch floured round biscuit cutter to cut out biscuits. Cut them as close together as possible. Transfer the biscuits to the baking sheet.

7. Brush the tops of the biscuits generously with the rice milk.

8. Bake in the center of the oven for 25 minutes, or until golden, rotating the pan halfway through.

9. Transfer the biscuits to a cooling rack. Serve warm.

Variation ■ **Herb Biscuits**: Add ¹/₄ cup finely chopped fresh herbs after you've cut in the shortening. Proceed with the recipe as written.

Flax Biscuits

MAKES 12 BISCUITS

Nutty golden flax adds omega-3s, lignans, and fiber to these savory biscuits, perfect with any meal. Have them for breakfast with vegan butter and jam, pair them up with soup for lunch, or pass them in the bread basket at dinner.

1³/4 cups plus 2 tablespoons rice milk

2 teaspoons freshly squeezed lemon juice

4 cups Basic Gluten-Free Flour Mix (page 19)

1 teaspoon xanthan gum

1 tablespoon plus 1 teaspoon double-acting baking powder

1 teaspoon baking soda

1 teaspoon salt

³/4 cup golden flaxseed meal

³/4 cup dairy-free, soy-free vegetable shortening, cut into tablespoon-sized pieces (chill a bit if it's not solid)

1 tablespoon rice milk mixed with 1 tablespoon canola oil

1. Combine the rice milk and lemon juice. Let sit for about 20 minutes.

2. Preheat the oven to 375°F. Line a baking sheet with parchment paper.

3. In a large bowl, whisk together the flour mix, xanthan gum, baking powder, baking soda, and salt. Add the flax meal and mix well.

4. Cut in the shortening, using a pastry blender, two knives, or your fingers, until you have a pea-sized crumb. Add the rice milk mixture, and stir until just combined, making sure you incorporate the crumbs at the bottom of the bowl.

5. Flour a work surface lightly with a little gluten-free flour mix, and turn out the dough. Lightly flour your hands. Sprinkle the dough with a little flour mix.

6. Gently pat the dough into a 1-inch-thick disk, pressing in any loose bits. Do not over-handle the dough.

7. Use a 2¹/2-inch floured round biscuit cutter to cut out biscuits. Cut them as close together as possible. Transfer the biscuits to the baking sheet. Gather together the scraps, and repeat until you've used up all the dough.

8. Brush the tops of the biscuits with the rice milk and oil mixture using a pastry brush.

9. Bake in the center of the oven for 25 minutes, or until golden. Transfer to a cooling rack. Serve warm.

Fennel Currant Drop Biscuits

MAKES 12 BISCUITS

Although the ingredients in this recipe may seem unusual, I urge you to give it a try. With their Mediterranean notes of fennel and olive oil, these biscuits taste festive and exotic.

1 1/2 cups quinoa flour
3/4 cup corn flour
1/2 teaspoon xanthan gum
2 teaspoons double-acting baking powder
1/2 teaspoon baking soda
1 teaspoon salt

1/2 cup dairy-free, soy-free vegetable
    shortening, chilled
2 tablespoons fennel seeds
1/2 cup currants
1 cup plain or vanilla vegan yogurt
1/4 cup extra virgin olive oil
1 tablespoon light agave nectar

1. Preheat the oven to 375°F. Line a baking sheet with parchment paper.

2. Whisk together the quinoa flour, corn flour, xanthan gum, baking powder, baking soda, and salt.

3. Cut in the shortening, using a pastry blender or two knives, until you have a pea-sized crumb.

4. Toss in 1 tablespoon of the fennel seeds and the currants.

5. Combine the yogurt with 2 tablespoons of the olive oil and the agave nectar, and add to the flour mixture. Stir until just combined, making sure you incorporate the crumbs at the bottom of the bowl.

6. With two large spoons, drop mounds of dough (about 1/4 cup each) about 1 1/2 inches apart on the baking sheet. You should be able to fit all 12 biscuits.

7. Brush the tops of the biscuits with the remaining 2 tablespoons olive oil and sprinkle with the remaining 1 tablespoon fennel seeds.

8. Bake in the center of the oven for 18 minutes, or until golden and aromatic. Transfer to a cooling rack. Serve warm.

Cinnamon Rolls

MAKES 12 ROLLS

These cinnamon rolls are to die for. I can hardly control myself as I wait for them to cool. In addition to their overwhelming yumminess, they are also incredibly easy to make. I've used rapid-rise yeast (also known as quick-rise yeast, fast-rising yeast, instant yeast, and/or bread machine yeast), which eliminates all that hanging around you normally do while waiting for old-fashioned slow-pokey yeast to rise. Make these for a holiday breakfast, or any weekend morning, for an extra somethin' special.

1 cup rice milk

1/4 cup canola oil

1/4 cup granulated sugar

2 1/4 cups Basic Gluten-Free Flour Mix (page 19)

1/2 teaspoon xanthan gum

2 teaspoons double-acting baking powder

1/2 teaspoon salt

1 (1/4-ounce) packet rapid-rise yeast

1/4 cup dairy-free, soy-free vegetable shortening

1/3 cup firmly packed light brown sugar

2 teaspoons ground cinnamon

1 recipe Rice Milk Glaze (recipe follows)

1. Combine the rice milk, canola oil, and granulated sugar in a microwave-safe measuring cup or bowl. Heat for about 1 minute until warm, but not hot (115°F). If the liquid is too hot, it will kill the yeast, so be careful.

2. In a large bowl, whisk together the flour mix, xanthan gum, baking powder, salt, and rapid-rise yeast.

3. Add the rice milk mixture to the dry mixture, and blend well. Cover with plastic wrap, and let rest for 10 minutes. Grease an 8-inch round pan.

4. Sprinkle your work surface and hands with ample gluten-free flour mix. Don't scrimp on the flour, or your dough will stick to the board. I usually use about 1/4 cup of flour mix. Turn out the dough onto the board, sprinkle with flour mix, pat down lightly, then flip.

5. Flour your rolling pin. Roll the dough into a long rectangle, 16 inches long and 9 inches wide (use your hands to coax it into shape, if necessary). It should be about 1/4 inch thick.

6. Soften the shortening by warming it in the microwave for about 30 seconds. Brush the shortening evenly over the top of the dough. Combine the light brown sugar and cinnamon, and sprinkle evenly across the dough.

7. Gently roll the dough lengthwise into a log. You may need to use a spatula to help coax it to turn at first (you should have a 16-inch log).

CONTINUED

CINNAMON ROLLS, *continued*

8. Cut the log into 12 pieces by first cutting the log in half, then into quarters, and then cutting each quarter into 3 pieces. Transfer the rolls to the pan. Cover tightly (I use plastic wrap, then put a rubber band around the top lip of the pan to secure the plastic). Place the pan in a dishpan and pour hot water to reach halfway up the sides of the pan (or just fill your kitchen sink basin). Let the rolls rise for 1 hour.

9. During the last 20 minutes of the rise, preheat the oven to 350°F.

10. Bake for 45 minutes, or until golden.

11. Drizzle with the glaze while still hot. Let cool in the pan until room temperature. Serve at room temperature.

Rice Milk Glaze

1 cup confectioners' sugar
1 tablespoon plus 1 1/2 teaspoons rice milk
1/2 teaspoon pure vanilla extract
1 1/2 teaspoons dairy-free, soy-free vegetable
    shortening, melted

Whisk all the ingredients together until smooth. Pour over the rolls. Let set.

Irish Soda Bread

MAKES 8 SERVINGS

This modern twist on a traditional favorite has the added benefit of being fat-free. That's right— no fat. So go ahead, dig in. I love this fresh out of the oven with a little vegan butter. It's also great toasted.

1/2 cup currants or raisins

3 tablespoons Irish whisky (optional, but celebratory of St. Patrick's Day)

1 (6-ounce) container plain or vanilla vegan yogurt

3/4 cup rice milk, plus extra for brushing top

1 tablespoon cider vinegar

3 cups Basic Gluten-Free Flour Mix (page 19)

3/4 teaspoon xanthan gum

1/3 cup firmly packed light brown sugar

1 tablespoon double-acting baking powder

1 teaspoon baking soda

1 teaspoon salt

1 tablespoon caraway seeds

1. Combine the currants and whisky and let soak for at least 1 hour.

2. Preheat the oven to 350°F. Line a baking sheet with parchment paper.

3. Whisk together the yogurt, 3/4 cup rice milk, and cider vinegar, and set aside.

4. In a large bowl, whisk together the flour mix, xanthan gum, light brown sugar, baking powder, baking soda, salt, and caraway seeds. Stir in the currants, whisky and all.

5. Add the rice milk mixture and stir with a wooden spoon until combined, being sure to mix in any crumbs at the bottom of the bowl.

6. Flour your hands with a little gluten-free flour mix. Turn the dough out onto the baking sheet. Mound into a dome shape, about 8 inches across.

7. Using a sharp knife, cut a cross shape into the loaf, about 3/4 inch deep.

8. Brush the top of the bread liberally with rice milk.

9. Bake in the center of the oven for 45 minutes, or until golden, rotating the pan halfway through. Transfer to a cooling rack (just slide the sheet of parchment paper from the baking sheet to the cooling rack).

Chocolate Zucchini Bread

MAKES 8 SERVINGS

This tasty quick bread is a great way to sneak vegetables into your kid's diet. When you combine chocolate and zucchini, the zucchini disappears. I tell my veggie-phobic son Lennon he's eating chocolate cake and he's none the wiser! He thinks he's really lucky to get chocolate cake for breakfast.

1/2 cup canola oil
1 cup light agave nectar
1 tablespoon pure vanilla extract
2 teaspoons ground cinnamon
2 cups grated/shredded zucchini
2 1/3 cups Basic Gluten-Free Flour Mix
  (page 19)

2/3 cup unsweetened cocoa powder
3/4 teaspoon xanthan gum
1 1/2 teaspoons baking soda
1/2 teaspoon salt
1 cup dairy-free, soy-free chocolate chips

1. Preheat the oven to 350°F. Grease a 9 by 5-inch loaf pan and sprinkle with a little gluten-free flour mix, tapping out any extra.

2. In the bowl of a stand mixer fitted with the paddle attachment, combine the canola oil and agave nectar, mixing on medium speed for 20 seconds.

3. Add the vanilla and cinnamon and mix.

4. Add the zucchini and mix until thoroughly combined, 20 seconds.

5. In a separate bowl, whisk together the flour mix, cocoa powder, xanthan gum, baking soda, and salt. Make sure you really mix it well, so that all lumps of cocoa powder are blended in.

6. Add the dry ingredients to the wet and mix on low speed until just combined, 20 seconds.

7. Fold in the chocolate chips.

8. Fill the loaf pan with batter and use the back of a spoon or a frosting spatula to smooth the surface.

9. Bake in the center of the oven for 55 to 60 minutes, rotating the pan halfway through. The bread is done when a skewer inserted into the center of the loaf comes out clean. Let cool in the pan for 10 minutes before transferring to a cooling rack.

Pumpkin Bread

MAKES 8 SERVINGS

With rich, tempting spices and a lovely autumnal hue, this bread is perfect during the harvest season.

1/2 cup canola oil

3/4 cup light agave nectar

1 teaspoon pure vanilla extract

1 1/2 cups (1 15-ounce can) pumpkin purée

1 teaspoon ground cinnamon

1/2 teaspoon ground nutmeg

1/4 teaspoon ground ginger

3 cups Basic Gluten-Free Flour Mix (page 19)

3/4 teaspoon xanthan gum

1 1/2 teaspoons baking soda

1/2 teaspoon salt

1/2 cup pumpkin seeds (optional)

1. Preheat the oven to 350°F. Grease a 9 by 5-inch loaf pan and sprinkle with a little gluten-free flour mix, tapping out any extra.

2. In the bowl of a stand mixer fitted with the paddle attachment, combine the canola oil, agave nectar, and vanilla, mixing on medium speed for 20 seconds.

3. Add the pumpkin, cinnamon, nutmeg, and ginger, and mix for 20 seconds.

4. In a separate bowl, whisk together the flour mix, xanthan gum, baking soda, and salt.

5. Add the dry ingredients to the wet and mix until combined, 30 seconds. Fold in the pumpkin seeds.

6. Fill the loaf pan with batter.

7. Bake in the center of the oven for 30 minutes, rotate the pan, reduce the temperature to 325°F, and bake for about 40 minutes more, or until lovely golden brown on top and a skewer inserted into the center of the loaf comes out clean. Let cool for about 20 minutes in the pan before transferring to a cooling rack.

Amaranth Date Bread

MAKES 8 SERVINGS

This simple quick bread is one of my favorites. It's wholesome and subtly sweet. Whole-grain amaranth has a nutty flavor, adds great texture, and is packed with protein and fiber.

1/2 cup whole-grain amaranth
1 cup boiling water
1 cup chopped dates
1/2 cup canola oil
1/2 cup light agave nectar
2 teaspoons pure vanilla extract
1 tablespoon Ener-G egg replacer mixed with
 1/4 cup rice milk

2 cups Basic Gluten-Free Flour Mix (page 19)
1 cup amaranth flour
3/4 teaspoon xanthan gum
1 tablespoon double-acting baking powder
1/2 teaspoon salt

1. In a pot, combine the amaranth and boiling water. Bring the amaranth to a boil, then reduce the heat to low and simmer for 15 minutes. Stir in the dates and turn off the heat. Let cool to room temperature.

2. Preheat the oven to 350°F. Grease a 9 by 5-inch loaf pan and sprinkle with a little gluten-free flour mix, tapping out any extra.

3. In the bowl of a stand mixer fitted with the paddle attachment, combine the canola oil and agave nectar, mixing on medium speed for 20 seconds. Add the vanilla and egg replacer. Mix for 20 seconds.

4. Whisk together the flour mix, amaranth flour, xanthan gum, baking powder, and salt.

5. Add the flour mixture to the wet ingredients and mix for about 20 seconds, until just combined. Add the dates and amaranth, and mix for about 1 minute. It will be thick.

6. Fill the loaf pan with batter and use the back of a spoon or a frosting spatula to smooth the surface.

7. Bake for 30 minutes, rotate the pan, reduce the temperature to 325°F, and bake for about 25 minutes more, or until golden and aromatic. Let cool for about 20 minutes in the pan before transferring to a cooling rack.

Blueberry Boy Bait

MAKES 8 SERVINGS

This moist, buttery coffee cake with its crisp, cinnamon-sugar topping is based on an old-fashioned recipe from the 1950s, called Blueberry Boy Bait, a coffee cake named for the effect it had on teenage boys. My boys aren't teens yet, but this bait works for them. They'll gobble it up in one day—with not a crumb left over.

2 cups Basic Gluten-Free Flour Mix (page 19)
1/2 teaspoon xanthan gum
1 tablespoon double-acting baking powder
1 teaspoon salt
3/4 cup dairy-free, soy-free vegetable shortening
3/4 cup firmly packed light brown sugar
1/2 cup granulated sugar

4 1/2 teaspoons Ener-G egg replacer mixed with
   6 tablespoons rice milk
3/4 cup rice milk
1 cup fresh or frozen blueberries tossed with
   1 tablespoon Basic Gluten-Free Flour Mix
1/4 cup granulated sugar mixed with
   1/2 teaspoon ground cinnamon

1. Preheat the oven to 350°F. Grease a 9 by 9-inch baking pan and sprinkle with a little gluten-free flour mix, tapping out any extra.

2. Whisk together the flour mix, xanthan gum, baking powder, and salt. Set aside.

3. In the bowl of a stand mixer fitted with the paddle attachment, combine the shortening, brown sugar, and granulated sugar. Mix on medium-high speed for 2 minutes, or until fluffy.

4. Add the egg replacer and mix for about 20 seconds.

5. Reduce the speed to medium and beat in one-third of the flour, mixing for 15 seconds.

6. Add half of the rice milk, mixing for 20 seconds.

7. Beat in half of the remaining flour, then the remaining rice milk, and finally the remaining flour mixture, scraping down the sides of the bowl as necessary.

8. Add half of the batter to the pan, using a frosting spatula to spread the batter evenly across the bottom of the pan. Sprinkle with half of the blueberries. Top with the remaining batter, spreading it as evenly as possible across the blueberries. Top with the remaining blueberries, then sprinkle with the cinnamon-sugar mixture.

9. Bake in the center of the oven for 1 hour, until the cinnamon-sugar mixture has begun to caramelize and the top is golden. Let cool in the pan for 30 minutes before turning out onto a serving platter (or just cut into pieces and serve out of the pan). Serve warm or at room temperature. This cake is even better on day two!

Tip ■ If using frozen blueberries, keep frozen until the last minute, or they'll turn your batter blue-green.

Classic Crumb Cake

MAKES 12 SERVINGS

I take this cake to meetings at my sons' school and wow the teachers. It's a conference room favorite. Nobody can believe it's vegan and gluten-free. It's straight-up classic coffee cake—moist and buttery, with a scrumptious crumb topping.

Crumb Topping
3/4 cup Basic Gluten-Free Flour Mix (page 19)
1/4 teaspoon xanthan gum
1/4 teaspoon kosher salt
1/2 cup firmly packed light brown sugar
1/2 teaspoon ground cinnamon
1/4 cup dairy-free, soy-free vegetable shortening, chilled and cut into tablespoon-size pieces

Cake
2 cups Basic Gluten-Free Flour Mix (page 19)
1/2 teaspoon xanthan gum
1 teaspoon double-acting baking powder
1 teaspoon baking soda
1 teaspoon salt
1 cup vanilla vegan yogurt
1 teaspoon cider vinegar
1/2 cup dairy-free, soy-free vegetable shortening, at room temperature
1 cup granulated sugar
1 tablespoon Ener-G egg replacer mixed with 1/4 cup rice milk
1 teaspoon pure vanilla extract
Confectioners' sugar, for dusting

1. Preheat the oven to 325°F. Grease a 9 by 9-inch baking pan and sprinkle with a little gluten-free flour mix, tapping out any extra.

2. To make the crumb topping, whisk together the flour mix, xanthan gum, and salt. Add the light brown sugar and cinnamon and whisk again. Add the chilled shortening, and using a pastry blender or two knives, blend until you have a pea-sized crumb. Set aside.

3. To make the cake, whisk together the flour mix, xanthan gum, baking powder, baking soda, and salt. Set aside.

4. Combine the vegan yogurt and cider vinegar. Set aside.

5. In the bowl of a stand mixer fitted with the paddle attachment, combine the shortening, granulated sugar, egg replacer, and vanilla. Beat on medium speed for about 2 minutes, or until light and fluffy. Add the flour mixture in three parts, alternating with the yogurt, beginning and ending with the flour. Beat until just combined, scraping down the sides of the bowl as necessary.

6. Spoon the batter into the prepared pan, smoothing out the surface. Sprinkle the crumb topping evenly over the top, using your fingers to clump some of it together into larger crumbs (think bakery aisle crumb coffee cake).

7. Bake in the center of the oven for 45 minutes, or until the top is golden and the cake springs back when touched lightly.

8. Let cool in the pan on a cooling rack for about 15 minutes. Invert the cake onto a large plate, cover with a cooling rack, and reinvert onto the rack crumb-side up. Let cool completely. Sift the confectioners' sugar over the top, and cut into squares. Store tightly covered at room temperature.

Linzer Hearts (page 73)

4

COOKIES

A cookie is the perfect treat: it's self-contained, easy to transport, and ideal any time of day. And, as far as I'm concerned, allergen-free cookies are even better than "normal" cookies. Yup, that's right, *better*. One of the very best things about allergen-free cookies is that the cookie dough is vegan, which means you can eat it raw! So I have provided proportions allowing for the fact that you or your baking assistants (aka kids) may sample as you bake, and still end up with two dozen cookies (or sixteen bars). These scrumptious little bites of heaven are also cholesterol-free, contain no hydrogenated fats, and are higher in fiber than your average cookie. But they still contain almost all of the traditional ingredients of cookie making—chocolate chips, chocolate chunks, cinnamon, raisins, decorating sugar, "cream" fillings, and jam. These cookies and bars all freeze well too, so feel free to bake them in bulk and store them in your freezer, defrosting whenever a cookie (or two or four!) strikes your fancy.

Classic Chocolate Chip Cookies

MAKES 24 2¹/₂-INCH COOKIES

I would argue that these fantastic cookies are even better than their traditional wheaty, eggy, buttery counterparts. The edges have that coveted toffee-like brown sugar crunch, and the inside is soft and chewy.

³/₄ cup dairy-free, soy-free vegetable shortening

¹/₂ cup plus 1 tablespoon granulated sugar

¹/₂ cup plus 1 tablespoon firmly packed light brown sugar

2¹/₄ teaspoons pure vanilla extract

2¹/₄ teaspoons Ener-G egg replacer mixed with 3 tablespoons rice milk

1¹/₂ cups plus 3 tablespoons Basic Gluten-Free Flour Mix (page 19)

³/₄ teaspoon xanthan gum

1¹/₈ teaspoons baking soda

¹/₂ teaspoon salt

1 cup plus 2 tablespoons dairy-free, soy-free chocolate chips

1. Preheat the oven to 350°F. Line two baking sheets with parchment paper.

2. In the bowl of a stand mixer fitted with the paddle attachment, cream the shortening, granulated sugar, and light brown sugar, mixing on medium speed until light and fluffy, about 2 minutes. Add the vanilla and egg replacer and mix for about 20 seconds, scraping down the sides of the bowl as necessary.

3. In a separate bowl, whisk together the flour mix, xanthan gum, baking soda, and salt.

4. Add the flour mixture to the creamed batter in two batches, mixing on low speed, just until the batter comes together, about 20 seconds.

5. Gently fold in the chocolate chips.

6. Drop by heaping tablespoons onto the baking sheets, 8 per sheet (3 down each side, 2 in the middle). Roll into balls, spacing the cookies a couple of inches apart. Flatten the cookies slightly with the palm of your hand. Bake for 11 minutes in the center of the oven, or until lightly golden around the edges. Let cool for 10 minutes on the baking sheet before transferring to a cooling rack. Repeat with the remaining dough.

Tip ■ **Beware of hot days**: they can turn your vegetable shortening into soup, resulting in a puddle of cookies. If your shortening is soft, put it in the fridge for an hour or so until it is solid again.

Double Choco Chunk Cookies

MAKES 24 2-INCH COOKIES

These chewy, brownielike cookies contain a double dose of chocolate and are full of Enjoy Life Boom Choco Boom chunks. They're perfect for every chocoholic (and I should know!).

1¼ cups Basic Gluten-Free Flour Mix
   (page 19)
½ cup unsweetened cocoa powder
½ teaspoon xanthan gum
½ teaspoon baking soda
1 teaspoon cream of tartar
¼ teaspoon salt
⅓ cup canola oil

⅓ cup rice milk
2 teaspoons pure vanilla extract
⅔ cup granulated sugar
1 cup Enjoy Life Rice Milk Boom Choco
   Boom bars, chopped into chunks (about
   4 [1.4-ounce] bars), or 1 cup dairy-free,
   soy-free chocolate chips

1. Preheat the oven to 325°F. Line two baking sheets with parchment paper.

2. Combine the flour mix, cocoa powder, xanthan gum, baking soda, cream of tartar, and salt. Mix thoroughly, being sure to work out any lumps of cocoa powder.

3. In the bowl of a stand mixer fitted with the paddle attachment, combine the canola oil and rice milk, mixing on medium speed for 30 seconds. Add the vanilla and sugar. Mix for 20 seconds.

4. Add the dry ingredients to the wet and mix on low speed, scraping down the sides of the bowl. Fold in the chocolate chunks.

5. Scoop out the dough by heaping tablespoonfuls and place on the baking sheets, 12 per sheet. Wet your hands with a little water and roll the dough into balls, moistening your hands again as necessary.

6. Bake in the center of the oven for 12 minutes, until just set. Do not overcook, as chocolate burns easily. You want the inside to remain chewy, not dry.

7. Let the cookies cool for 5 minutes on the baking sheets before transferring to a cooling rack.

Chocolate Sandwich Cookies

MAKES 24 2-INCH COOKIES

These are my son Lennon's favorite cookies. They're like a soft Oreo, but unlike Oreos, where most kids just break them open, eat the cream filling, and discard the hard cookie exterior, Lennon ooohs and ahs and chows down the whole thing. Store them in a tightly sealed container and they'll last well for days.

Cookies

1/2 cup plus 1 tablespoon dairy-free, soy-free vegetable shortening

3/4 cup granulated sugar

2 teaspoons pure vanilla extract

3 tablespoons unsweetened applesauce

1 1/2 teaspoons Ener-G egg replacer mixed with 2 tablespoons rice milk

1 1/2 cups Basic Gluten-Free Flour Mix (page 19)

3/4 teaspoon xanthan gum

1/4 cup plus 3 tablespoons unsweetened cocoa powder

3/4 teaspoon double-acting baking powder

3/4 teaspoon baking soda

1/8 teaspoon salt

Cream Filling

2 tablespoons dairy-free, soy-free vegetable shortening

1 1/2 cups confectioners' sugar

1/2 teaspoon pure vanilla extract

1 1/2 tablespoons hot water

1. To make the cookies, in the bowl of a stand mixer fitted with the paddle attachment, combine the shortening and sugar, mixing on medium speed. Beat until light and fluffy, about 2 minutes. Add the vanilla, applesauce, and egg replacer. Mix for about 30 seconds.

2. Whisk together the flour mix, xanthan gum, cocoa powder, baking powder, baking soda, and salt.

3. Add the dry ingredients to the wet and mix until smooth, about 20 seconds.

4. Lay out two sheets of plastic wrap, each about 15 inches long. Divide the dough in half. Place half of the dough on each sheet of plastic wrap. Fold the plastic wrap over the dough, and shape it into a log 6 inches long and 2 inches in diameter. Flatten the ends of the log, and wrap the plastic wrap at each end, folding it over tightly. Put the log in the fridge to chill. Repeat with the other half of dough. Let chill for at least 2 hours. If the dough still needs firming, put the logs in the freezer for about 15 minutes. It needs to be firm to slice easily.

5. Preheat the oven to 325°F. Line two baking sheets with parchment paper.

6. Remove one log from the fridge. Roll it on the counter to reshape, if necessary. Unwrap, and using a thin sharp knife, cut into 24 1/4-inch slices. I do this by cutting the log in

CONTINUED

half, then into quarters, then cutting each quarter into 6 slices. Place the cookies about 1 inch apart (you can fit 24 on one sheet). Bake in the center of the oven for 9 minutes, until just set around the edges. Remove from the oven, and let cool on the baking sheet for 5 minutes before transferring to a cooling rack to cool completely.

7. Repeat with the other log of dough.

8. To make the cream filling, combine all the filling ingredients in the bowl of a stand mixer fitted with the paddle attachment, mixing on medium speed. Beat until smooth and creamy. If it is not creamy enough to spread easily, add a little more hot water, $1/2$ teaspoon at a time, until it reaches a very smooth consistency. Spread the filling on one side of a cookie and cover with another cookie.

9. Store in an airtight container.

Variation ■ **Chocolate Mint Sandwich Cookies**: Add a dash of peppermint extract to the cream filling, a little at a time, to taste.

Snickerdoodles

MAKES 24 2$^1/_2$-INCH COOKIES

When I give these to vegan friends, they think they've died and gone to heaven. Nobody can believe they're vegan and gluten-free. They disappear as fast as I can bake them, so I make them in bulk and keep them in the freezer.

2$^1/_2$ cups plus 2 tablespoons Basic Gluten-Free Flour Mix (page 19)

$^1/_2$ teaspoon plus $^1/_8$ teaspoon xanthan gum

$^3/_4$ teaspoon baking soda

1$^1/_2$ teaspoons cream of tartar

$^1/_4$ teaspoon salt

$^3/_4$ cup dairy-free, soy-free vegetable shortening

$^3/_4$ cup granulated sugar

$^1/_4$ cup plus 2 tablespoons firmly packed brown sugar

2 teaspoons pure vanilla extract

1$^1/_2$ teaspoons Ener-G egg replacer mixed with 2 tablespoons rice milk

$^1/_4$ cup plus 1 teaspoon rice milk

2 tablespoons granulated sugar mixed with 2 teaspoons ground cinnamon

1. Preheat the oven to 375°F. Line two baking sheets with parchment paper.

2. Whisk together the flour mix, xanthan gum, baking soda, cream of tartar, and salt.

3. In the bowl of a stand mixer fitted with the paddle attachment, combine the shortening, granulated sugar, and brown sugar, mixing on medium speed until fluffy, about 2 minutes. Add the vanilla and egg replacer. Mix for 20 seconds.

4. Add the flour mixture in two batches, mixing on low speed, alternating with the rice milk, and scraping down the sides of the bowl as necessary.

5. Roll the dough into 24 heaping tablespoon–size balls (1$^1/_2$ inches in diameter). Roll the balls in the cinnamon-sugar mixture until coated on all sides (they'll look like Dunkin' Donuts cinnamon Munchkins!).

6. Place on the baking sheets 3 inches apart. Bake for 10 minutes in the center of the oven. Let cool for 10 minutes on the baking sheets before transferring to a cooling rack.

Chocolate Thumbprint Cookies

MAKES 24 2-INCH COOKIES

Pretty and elegant, these cookies will make your mouth water, and they're fun to make! Kids love sticking their thumb in the middle of the cookies, and filling the mini pool with creamy delicious chocolate. See below for a fruity variation.

1¼ cups plus 1 tablespoon Basic Gluten-Free Flour Mix (page 19)

¼ teaspoon plus ⅛ teaspoon xanthan gum

¼ teaspoon plus ⅛ teaspoon baking soda

¾ teaspoon cream of tartar

⅛ teaspoon salt

¼ cup plus 2 tablespoons dairy-free, soy-free vegetable shortening

¼ cup plus 2 tablespoons granulated sugar

3 tablespoons firmly packed brown sugar

¾ teaspoon pure vanilla extract

¾ teaspoon Ener-G egg replacer mixed with 1 tablespoon rice milk

2 tablespoons plus ¾ teaspoon rice milk

½ cup dairy-free, soy-free chocolate chips

1. Preheat the oven to 350°F. Line two baking sheets with parchment paper.

2. Whisk together the flour mix, xanthan gum, baking soda, cream of tartar, and salt.

3. In the bowl of a stand mixer fitted with the paddle attachment, combine the shortening, granulated sugar, and brown sugar, mixing on medium speed until fluffy, about 2 minutes, and scraping down the sides of the bowl as necessary. Add the vanilla and egg replacer. Mix for 20 seconds.

4. Add the flour mixture to the creamed batter in three batches, alternating with the rice milk, mixing on low speed and scraping down the sides of the bowl as necessary.

5. Scoop out the dough by 2 teaspoonfuls and place on the baking sheets, 12 per sheet. Wet your hands with a little water and roll the dough into balls.

6. Bake in the center of the oven for 5 minutes.

7. Put the chocolate chips in a microwave-safe bowl and melt. This will take about 1 minute; check the chips halfway through and stir. Once the chips are melted, set them aside.

8. Remove the cookies from the oven. Wet your thumb with cool water and, working quickly, make thumbprint marks in the center of each cookie. Fill the thumbprints with ½ teaspoon of melted chocolate.

9. Return the cookies to the oven and bake an additional 5 to 6 minutes, or until set.

10. Let the cookies cool for 5 minutes on the baking sheets before transferring to a cooling rack.

Variation ■ **Jammy Thumbprint Cookies:** Fill thumbprints with ½ teaspoon jam instead of chocolate. Raspberry, strawberry, and apricot all work very well for this.

Thin and Crispy Oatmeal Cookies

MAKES 24 3-INCH COOKIES

I don't know what to call these, other than perfect. But don't thank me, thank the advent of gluten-free oats. Hurray for oats! This is my favorite cookie.

1¼ cups Basic Gluten-Free Flour Mix
(page 19)
½ teaspoon xanthan gum
¾ teaspoon double-acting baking powder
½ teaspoon baking soda
½ teaspoon salt
¾ cup plus 2 tablespoons dairy-free, soy-free
vegetable shortening

1 cup granulated sugar
¼ cup firmly packed light brown sugar
3 tablespoons warm water mixed with
1 tablespoon flaxseed meal ("flax egg")
1 teaspoon pure vanilla extract
2½ cups gluten-free old-fashioned oats

1. Preheat the oven to 325°F. Line two baking sheets with parchment paper.

2. Whisk together the flour mix, xanthan gum, baking powder, baking soda, and salt in a medium bowl.

3. In the bowl of a stand mixer fitted with the paddle attachment, combine the shortening, granulated sugar, and brown sugar, mixing on low speed for about 20 seconds. Increase the speed to medium and continue beating for about 1 minute longer, or until light and fluffy.

4. Add the "flax egg" and vanilla and mix to combine, about 20 seconds. Scrape down the sides of the bowl.

5. Add the flour mixture and beat on low speed until just combined.

6. Add the oats and mix on low speed for about 20 seconds.

7. Use a 2-tablespoon scoop (either a #30 cookie scoop or a coffee scoop) to scoop out the dough and place on the baking sheet. Roll the scooped dough into balls, spacing them about 2½ inches apart on the baking sheet. This works best if you put 3 down each side and 2 in the middle. Flatten the cookies into disks with the palm of your hand, the thinner the better.

8. Bake in the center of the oven for 18 minutes, or until lightly golden, rotating the baking sheet halfway through. Transfer the baking sheet to a cooling rack. Let cool for about 5 minutes before transferring the cookies to the rack. Let cool completely. Repeat with the remaining dough.

Chocolate Chip Oatmeal Raisin Cookies

MAKES 24 2½-INCH COOKIES

A hearty, chewy classic! Pack these in your kids' lunch for a snack, or serve them after school with a big chilled glass of rice milk for dunking!

½ cup dairy-free, soy-free vegetable shortening
½ cup granulated sugar
¼ cup firmly packed brown sugar
1 teaspoon pure vanilla extract
¾ teaspoon Ener-G egg replacer mixed with
    1 tablespoon rice milk
1¼ cups Basic Gluten-Free Flour Mix
    (page 19)

½ teaspoon xanthan gum
½ teaspoon baking soda
⅛ teaspoon salt
3 tablespoons rice milk
1 cup gluten-free old-fashioned oats
½ cup dairy-free, soy-free chocolate chips
½ cup raisins

1. Preheat the oven to 350°F. Line two baking sheets with parchment paper.

2. In the bowl of a stand mixer fitted with the paddle attachment, cream the shortening, granulated sugar, and brown sugar, mixing on medium speed for about 1 minute. Add the vanilla and egg replacer and mix for 20 seconds.

3. In a separate bowl, whisk together the flour mix, xanthan gum, baking soda, and salt.

4. Add the flour mixture to the mixer in three batches, mixing on low speed, alternating with the rice milk.

5. Add the oats, chocolate chips, and raisins. Mix on the lowest possible speed until just combined. Use a wooden spoon or rubber spatula to finish blending, if necessary.

6. Drop by rounded tablespoons onto the baking sheets, spacing them 3 inches apart. Bake for 12 minutes in the center of the oven, or until lightly golden around the edges. Let cool for 5 minutes on the baking sheets before transferring to a cooling rack.

Chocolate Sandwich Cookies (page 57),
Chocolate Chip Oatmeal Raisin Cookies (opposite),
and Snickerdoodles (page 59)

Old-Fashioned Oatmeal Lace Cookies

MAKES 24 4-INCH COOKIES

My grandmother Catherene used to make a version of these when I was a child. I still remember waiting in the kitchen for them to set, barely able to contain myself as their tempting aroma wafted through the house.

1/2 cup dairy-free, soy-free vegetable shortening

1/2 cup firmly packed light brown sugar

1/4 cup granulated sugar

1/4 cup molasses

1 teaspoon pure vanilla extract

1 1/2 teaspoons Ener-G egg replacer mixed with 2 tablespoons rice milk

1 cup Basic Gluten-Free Flour Mix (page 19)

1/4 teaspoon xanthan gum

1/4 teaspoon salt

1/2 teaspoon ground cinnamon

1/2 teaspoon baking soda dissolved in 1 tablespoon water

1 1/2 cups gluten-free old-fashioned oats

1/2 cup chopped dates or raisins

1. Preheat the oven to 350°F. Line two baking sheets with parchment paper.

2. In the bowl of a stand mixer fitted with the paddle attachment, combine the shortening, brown sugar, granulated sugar, and molasses. Mix on medium speed for 1 minute. Add the vanilla and egg replacer and mix until combined, about 20 seconds.

3. Whisk together the flour mix, xanthan gum, salt, and cinnamon. Add to the creamed batter along with the baking soda dissolved in water. Mix on low speed for 30 seconds, scraping down the sides of the bowl as necessary. Add the oats, stir with a wooden spoon or rubber spatula, then stir in the dates.

4. Drop by heaping teaspoonfuls onto the baking sheet, 6 per sheet.

5. Bake for 11 to 12 minutes in the center of the oven, or until the cookies are browning around the edges.

6. Transfer the cookies to a cooling rack by quickly sliding the parchment paper sideways off the baking sheet onto the rack. Let cool to room temperature. The cookies will turn crisp and lacey. Store tightly covered in single layers separated by parchment paper or waxed paper.

Orange Spritz Cookies

MAKES 120 1^1/$_2$-INCH COOKIES

Spritz cookies are the backbone of holiday baking. You can decorate them with any kind of sprinkles, drizzle them with chocolate, dust them with sparkly sugars, add food coloring to make them in a rainbow of colors, press them out into any shape . . . they're endlessly versatile. I've spruced up the classic recipe slightly by adding a hint of orange flavor, giving them just a little special oomph. I've written proportions for a large batch so you can give them as gifts or make them for a party. They also store well in the freezer, so you can keep them on hand for treats anytime.

1^1/$_2$ cups dairy-free, soy-free vegetable shortening	1 teaspoon orange zest
1 cup granulated sugar	2 tablespoons orange juice
1 teaspoon double-acting baking powder	3^1/$_2$ cups Basic Gluten-Free Flour Mix (page 19)
1^1/$_2$ teaspoons Ener-G egg replacer mixed with	^{3}/$_4$ teaspoon xanthan gum
2 tablespoons rice milk	^{1}/$_4$ teaspoon salt
1 teaspoon pure vanilla extract	Decorative sugars, sprinkles, etc. (optional)

1. Preheat the oven to 350°F.

2. In the bowl of a stand mixer fitted with the paddle attachment, combine the shortening and granulated sugar, mixing on medium speed for about 30 seconds. Add the baking powder and mix until combined, about 10 seconds. Mix in the egg replacer, vanilla, orange zest, and orange juice until combined, about 30 seconds.

3. In a separate bowl, whisk together the flour mix, xanthan gum, and salt.

4. Add the flour mixture to the shortening mixture, beating on low speed until combined.

5. Pack the dough into a cookie press. Place the face of the press firmly down on an ungreased baking sheet. Press out a cookie. Space the cookies about 1 inch apart. Decorate with colored sugar.

6. Bake for 8 minutes in the center of the oven, or until the cookie edges are firm but not brown. Cool on the baking sheet for a couple of minutes before transferring to a cooling rack.

Tip ■ The key to perfect spritz cookies is mastering a cookie press. Try the Wilton Comfort Grip Cookie Press (www.wilton.com). The rule: a single press, a pretty cookie. (A double press makes a messy blob.) Test-press a few cookies to get the knack of it, and to get the dough moving. Then you're off and pressing!

    If the dough is too soft (if it's a very warm day, this may happen), put it in the fridge for about 30 minutes to firm it up. But please note, under normal conditions, this dough does not call for chilling.

    Also, make sure your baking sheets aren't warped. If you're baking sheets aren't flat, your cookie press will rebel.

Rolled Brown Sugar Cookies

MAKES 24 3-INCH COOKIES

Make these for any of the holidays where you want cutout cookies. They're perfect for Halloween, Christmas and Hanukkah, Valentine's Day, Easter . . . you get the idea. They're also great made into letter cookies or animals. My kids love baking these as an activity. It's part cooking, part art project, and they're so proud of their handiwork once it comes out of the oven.

Cookies

2 1/2 cups plus 2 tablespoons Basic Gluten-Free Flour Mix (page 19), plus more for sprinkling

1/2 teaspoon plus 1/8 teaspoon xanthan gum

3/4 teaspoon baking soda

1/4 teaspoon salt

3/4 cup dairy-free, soy-free vegetable shortening

3/4 cup granulated sugar

1/4 cup plus 2 tablespoons firmly packed brown sugar

1 1/2 teaspoons pure vanilla extract

1 1/2 teaspoons Ener-G egg replacer mixed with 2 tablespoons rice milk

3 tablespoons rice milk

White Icing

3 cups confectioners' sugar

3 tablespoons rice milk (add a little more if necessary)

Sprinkles, decorating sugar, etc.

1. To make the cookies, whisk together the flour mix, xanthan gum, baking soda, and salt.

2. In the bowl of a stand mixer fitted with the paddle attachment, combine the shortening, granulated sugar, and brown sugar, mixing on medium speed until fully combined, about 2 minutes. Add the vanilla and egg replacer and mix for about 20 seconds, or until combined.

3. Add the flour mixture to the bowl in three batches, mixing on low speed, alternating with the rice milk, and scraping down the sides of the bowl as necessary.

4. Divide the dough into two balls. Form into disks, wrap in waxed paper or plastic wrap, and refrigerate for 2 hours. Do not refrigerate overnight.

5. Preheat the oven to 350°F. Line two baking sheets with parchment paper.

6. Sprinkle an ample amount of flour mix on your work surface and rolling pin. Remove one disk of dough from the fridge. Pat a little of the flour mix onto both sides of the dough. Flatten the disk with the palm of your hand. Roll out the dough to 1/4 inch thick. (It may be a little stiff at first but will soften up fast. Pinch the edges together with your fingers the first go-around, if necessary.) Sprinkle more flour mix as needed to prevent the dough from sticking as you roll it out.

7. Using 3-inch cookie cutters, cut out the dough into desired shapes. Transfer the cookies to the baking sheet. Gather the remaining scraps and repeat.

8. Bake in the center of the oven for 10 minutes, or until just slightly golden. Let cool for 10 minutes on the baking sheet before transferring to a cooling rack to cool completely.

9. To make the icing, combine the confectioners' sugar and rice milk and beat with an electric mixer until smooth.

10. Spread icing on one cooled cookie at a time. Quickly sprinkle it with decorating sugar before icing the next cookie. Repeat with each cookie until finished. Store covered. These cookies will keep well in the fridge for days, and they also freeze very well.

CHILLING ALLERGEN-FREE DOUGH

Please do not chill these cookie doughs overnight, as they will become dry and brittle. Because the dough has no gluten or eggs, it will become too stiff sitting in the fridge that long and will be impossible to work with correctly. So if a recipe calls for chilling 2 hours before rolling it out, please stick to 2 hours, not 24.

Ginger Snaps

MAKES 24 1¹/₂-INCH COOKIES

This recipe first appeared in Living Without *in December 2008. I had to include it here because it's so good, and also because it reminds me of my grandmother Catherene, who taught me to bake cookies. She was very fond of ginger.*

¹/₄ cup dairy-free, soy-free vegetable shortening

¹/₄ cup granulated sugar, plus 2 tablespoons for rolling cookies in

2 tablespoons light brown sugar

2 tablespoons molasses

2 tablespoons bitter orange marmalade

¹/₂ teaspoon pure vanilla extract

1 cup Basic Gluten-Free Flour Mix (page 19)

¹/₄ teaspoon xanthan gum

¹/₄ teaspoon baking soda

¹/₂ teaspoon cream of tartar

¹/₈ teaspoon salt

1 teaspoon ground ginger

¹/₂ teaspoon ground cinnamon

¹/₄ teaspoon ground nutmeg

1. Preheat the oven to 350°F. Line two baking sheets with parchment paper.

2. In the bowl of a stand mixer fitted with the paddle attachment, combine the shortening and ¹/₄ cup of the granulated sugar, mixing on medium speed until smooth and fluffy, about 1 minute. Add the brown sugar, molasses, orange marmalade, and vanilla. Mix thoroughly, 2 minutes.

3. In a separate bowl, whisk together the flour mix, xanthan gum, baking soda, cream of tartar, salt, ginger, cinnamon, and nutmeg.

4. Add the flour mixture to the shortening mixture and beat on low speed to combine, scraping down the sides of the bowl as necessary.

5. Using your hands, roll teaspoon-size pieces of dough into balls.

6. Pour the remaining 2 tablespoons of granulated sugar into a shallow bowl or plate. Roll the balls in the sugar and place on the parchment paper.

7. Bake in the center of the oven for 14 minutes, until puffed into perfect little domes and just starting to crack.

8. Let cool for about 5 minutes on the baking sheets before transferring to a cooling rack to cool completely.

Gingerbread Boys

MAKES 24 3-INCH COOKIES

These chewy gingerbread cookies contain half the fat of most traditional gingerbread recipes, have no cholesterol, and swap out the sugar for agave nectar and molasses. But do they sacrifice on flavor? No way! My boys say, "They're better than great!"

3³/4 cups Basic Gluten-Free Flour Mix (page 19)
1 teaspoon xanthan gum
³/4 teaspoon baking soda
1 teaspoon salt
1 tablespoon ground cinnamon
1 tablespoon ground ginger
¹/2 teaspoon ground cloves

¹/2 cup dairy-free, soy-free vegetable shortening, cut into about 8 pieces
¹/2 cup unsweetened applesauce
¹/2 cup light agave nectar
¹/4 cup plus 2 tablespoons molasses
Currants; raisins; dairy-free, soy-free chocolate chips; decorating sugar, etc.

1. In the bowl of a stand mixer fitted with the paddle attachment, combine the flour mix, xanthan gum, baking soda, salt, cinnamon, ginger, and cloves. Mix on low speed until combined, about 30 seconds. Stop the mixer, add the pieces of shortening and the applesauce, then mix on low speed for about 1¹/2 minutes, or until the consistency of a fine meal.

2. With the mixer still running, add the agave nectar and molasses, mixing until thoroughly combined, about 20 more seconds. (If you don't have a standing mixer, use a food processor, adding ingredients as instructed, and process for about 10 seconds between each step.)

3. Lay out two large sheets of parchment paper on your work surface. Using a rubber spatula, divide the dough evenly between the two sheets. Cover each with another large sheet of parchment paper and roll out with a rolling pin to ¹/4 inch thick.

4. Transfer the dough in the parchment paper to the freezer and chill until firm, at least 20 minutes (you'll want to clear a couple of racks, or chill the dough on trays).

5. Preheat the oven to 350°F. Line two baking sheets with parchment paper.

6. Remove one sheet of dough from the freezer and place on the work surface. Peel back the top sheet of parchment paper, then replace it. Flip, peel off the other sheet of parchment paper, and discard it.

7. Cut the dough into 3-inch gingerbread boys. Transfer to the baking sheet using a thin metal spatula, spacing them about 1 inch apart. Set the scraps aside.

8. Repeat the process with the remaining dough, and decorate the cookies with currants, chocolate chips, colorful sparkling sugar, or anything else you fancy.

9. Bake in the center of the oven for 10 minutes, or until set. Do not overbake. Remove from the oven, let cool for a couple of minutes on the baking sheets, then transfer to a cooling rack to cool completely.

SunButter Greenies

MAKES 24 3-INCH COOKIES

This cookie was a happy accident. I was experimenting with SunButter and discovered that when you bake it combined with maple syrup, it turns the center of the cookie green. (It has to cool to work its alchemy.) My husband loves these cookies because they have no refined sugar, and my kids like them for their Dr. Seuss–like hue. They're perfect for the Christmas season or as a healthy snack all year round. Use organic unsweetened SunButter if you can find it; if not, regular works fine, too. Be sure to measure the SunButter and the maple syrup with a liquid measuring cup. Remember there is a small chance of soy cross-contamination with SunButter (see page 179 for more information), but if that's a problem you can make your own sunflower seed butter.

2 cups plus 4 tablespoons Basic Gluten-Free Flour Mix (page 19)
1/2 teaspoon xanthan gum
1 teaspoon baking soda
1 teaspoon salt

1 1/2 cups SunButter
1 1/2 cups pure maple syrup
2 teaspoons pure vanilla extract
1 1/2 cups dairy-free, soy-free chocolate chips

1. Preheat the oven to 350°F. Line two baking sheets with parchment paper.

2. In a medium bowl, combine the flour mix, xanthan gum, baking soda, and salt. Mix well.

3. Put the SunButter in a microwave-safe glass measuring cup or bowl. Heat for about 1 minute in the microwave, or until softened.

4. Add the softened SunButter, maple syrup, and vanilla to the dry ingredients in the mixing bowl. Mix well with a wooden spoon. Once combined, stir in the chocolate chips.

5. Drop 2 tablespoons of dough for each cookie onto the baking sheets, then flatten the cookies slightly with the back of a clean spoon.

6. Bake for 15 minutes in the center of the oven, until lightly golden.

7. Let cool for about 5 minutes on the baking sheets before transferring to a cooling rack to cool completely. The cookies must cool all the way to turn green in the center.

Tip ■ You can buy a 2-tablespoon scoop at most cooking supply stores. They are often sold as coffee scoops.

Orange Marmalade Tea Biscuits

MAKES 24 2-INCH BISCUITS

These diminutive tea biscuits are a wonderful little treat. My son Lennon, upon tasting them, told me he'd like to take them with him to heaven. Really, he said that. Just a little word of caution: these puppies are hot, so wait until they've cooled a bit to eat them, or the orange marmalade will scorch the roof of your mouth.

3 cups Basic Gluten-Free Flour Mix (page 19)
3/4 teaspoon xanthan gum
2 tablespoons double-acting baking powder
3/4 teaspoon salt
6 tablespoons dairy-free, soy-free vegetable
  shortening

1 1/2 teaspoons Ener-G egg replacer mixed
  with 2 tablespoons rice milk
1 cup orange marmalade
1/2 cup rice milk

1. Preheat the oven to 400°F. Line two baking sheets with parchment paper.

2. In the bowl of a stand mixer fitted with the paddle attachment, combine the flour mix, xanthan gum, baking powder, and salt, mixing on medium speed for 20 seconds.

3. Add the shortening and mix on low speed until you have a coarse meal, about 1 minute.

4. With the mixer still running, add the egg replacer, then 1/2 cup of the marmalade, then the rice milk. Mix until the dough is just combined. It will still be crumbly.

5. Sprinkle your work surface, a rolling pin, and your hands with a little gluten-free flour mix. Turn out the dough onto the floured board, pat into a disk, and gently roll out the dough to about 1/2 inch thick.

6. Cut with a 2-inch floured biscuit cutter, gathering scraps and rerolling as necessary. Place 12 biscuits on each baking sheet. Top each with about 1 teaspoon of the remaining marmalade. Bake for 15 minutes, until the biscuits are lightly golden around the edges and the marmalade is bubbling. Let cool slightly before eating.

Lemon Madeleines

MAKES 24 MADELEINES

There's an old French saying that madeleines are supposed to take one back to one's childhood. So transport yourself back in time, or begin the tradition anew with your little ones. These small, light, lemony, shell-shaped sponge cakes are easy to make; you just need the proper pan. They are perfect with a cup of tea or for breakfast with a glass of rice milk.

1/2 cup dairy-free, soy-free vegetable shortening

2 tablespoons Ener-G egg replacer mixed with 1/2 cup rice milk

1 1/2 cups granulated sugar

4 teaspoons freshly squeezed lemon juice

2 teaspoons pure vanilla extract

2 teaspoons natural yellow food coloring (optional, but pretty—try Seelect made with turmeric)

2 teaspoons lemon zest

2 cups Basic Gluten-Free Flour Mix (page 19)

1/2 teaspoon xanthan gum

1 teaspoon baking soda

1/2 teaspoon salt

1/2 cup vanilla vegan yogurt

Confectioners' sugar, for dusting

1. Preheat the oven to 400°F. Grease your madeleine pan.

2. Melt the shortening in a small microwave-safe bowl and set aside.

3. In the bowl of a stand mixer fitted with the paddle attachment, combine the egg replacer, granulated sugar, lemon juice, vanilla, and yellow food coloring. Mix on low speed to combine, about 20 seconds, then increase the speed to high and beat until very light and lemon colored, about 2 minutes. Mix in the lemon zest on low speed, about 10 seconds.

4. In a separate bowl, whisk together the flour mix, xanthan gum, baking soda, and salt.

5. Add the melted shortening to the mixer, and combine on low speed for about 20 seconds. Add the flour mixture, then the yogurt. Beat until smooth.

6. Spoon a scant 1 1/2 tablespoons batter into each madeleine shell, and smooth down to fill the shell, using a butter knife or the back of a spoon. Do not overfill the shells or they will overflow when they rise in the oven.

7. Bake for 18 to 20 minutes, or until golden. Immediately remove the madeleines from the shells to a cooling rack by inserting a butter knife under one end, and flipping the madeleines out onto the rack, ridged side up.

8. Repeat until all the batter is used, greasing the madeleine pan each time.

9. Once they've cooled to room temperature, sift a little confectioners' sugar over the tops. Store tightly covered if not serving right away, though they're best when fresh. They also freeze well.

Linzer Hearts

MAKES 24 COOKIES (12 3-INCH SANDWICH COOKIES AND 12 2-INCH HEARTS)

Sophisticated and divine, these cookies are a real treat, whether it's Valentine's Day or you just feel like saying "I love you." And, they're made without the traditional allergenic addition of hazelnuts or almonds; what could be better?

2¹/₂ cups plus 2 tablespoons Basic Gluten-Free Flour Mix (page 19)

¹/₂ teaspoon plus ¹/₈ teaspoon xanthan gum

³/₄ teaspoon baking soda

¹/₄ teaspoon salt

¹/₂ teaspoon ground cinnamon

³/₄ cup dairy-free, soy-free vegetable shortening

³/₄ cup granulated sugar

¹/₄ cup plus 2 tablespoons firmly packed brown sugar

1¹/₂ teaspoons pure vanilla extract

¹/₂ teaspoon lemon zest

1¹/₂ teaspoons Ener-G egg replacer mixed with 2 tablespoons rice milk

3 tablespoons rice milk

¹/₂ cup raspberry jam

Confectioners' sugar, for dusting

1. Whisk together the flour mix, xanthan gum, baking soda, salt, and cinnamon.

2. In the bowl of a stand mixer fitted with the paddle attachment, combine the shortening, granulated sugar, and brown sugar on medium speed, beating until fluffy, about 2 minutes. Add the vanilla, lemon zest, and egg replacer. Mix for about 20 seconds.

3. Add the flour mixture to the bowl in three batches, mixing on low, alternating with the rice milk, and scraping down the sides of the bowl as necessary, until the dough comes together.

4. Divide the dough into two balls. Form into disks, wrap in waxed paper or plastic wrap, and refrigerate for 2 hours.

5. Line two baking sheets with parchment paper.

6. Sprinkle flour mix on your work surface and your rolling pin. Remove one disk of dough from the fridge. Sprinkle a little of the flour mix onto both sides of the dough. Use the palm of your hand to flatten the disk, then roll out the dough to ¹/₈ inch thick. (It will be a little stiff at first but will soften up fast. Pinch the edges together with your fingers the first go-around, if necessary.)

7. Cut into 12 heart shapes using a 3-inch heart-shaped cookie cutter. Cut out the center from half the shapes with a 2-inch heart-shaped cookie cutter. Using a metal spatula, carefully transfer the shapes to the baking sheet, about 1 inch apart. Repeat with the remaining dough and scraps until you have 12 whole hearts, 12 hearts with the centers cut out, and about 12 bite-size hearts. Put the baking sheets in the fridge to chill the cookies again.

CONTINUED

8. Preheat the oven to 325°F.

9. Bake in the center of the oven for 15 minutes, or until just slightly golden, rotating the pan halfway through. Let cool for 10 minutes on the baking sheet before transferring to a cooling rack to cool completely.

10. Once the cookies have cooled, spread the large whole hearts with the raspberry jam. Sift the confectioners' sugar over the hearts with the centers cut out and the small bite-size hearts. Top the large whole hearts with an open heart.

Cranberry Chocolate Chip Biscotti

MAKES 24 COOKIES

Subtly sweet and ultra-crispy, these twice-baked Italian cookies are an all-purpose treat. Great for dipping, dunking, or just plain snacking, they're wonderful to have on hand any time of day. I like mine dunked in tea, and my kids like theirs partnered with vegan ice cream.

3 cups Basic Gluten-Free Flour Mix (page 19)

3/4 teaspoon xanthan gum

2 teaspoons double-acting baking powder

1/4 teaspoon salt

5 tablespoons plus 1/2 cup orange juice

1/4 cup cornstarch

1 cup plus 2 tablespoons granulated sugar

2 tablespoons canola oil

2 teaspoons pure vanilla extract

1/2 cup dried cranberries

1/3 cup dairy-free, soy-free chocolate chips

1 tablespoon rice milk

1. Preheat the oven to 325°F. Line a baking sheet with parchment paper.

2. Whisk together the flour mix, xanthan gum, baking powder, and salt. Set aside.

3. In a small bowl, whisk together 5 tablespoons of the orange juice with the cornstarch. Set aside.

4. In the bowl of a stand mixer fitted with the paddle attachment, combine 1 cup of the sugar with the remaining 1/2 cup orange juice, mixing on medium speed for about 20 seconds. Add the canola oil and vanilla and mix for about 1 minute. Add the cornstarch mixture, and mix until combined, about 20 seconds.

5. Add the flour mixture in two batches, mixing on low speed. Fold in the cranberries and chocolate chips using either a wooden spoon or a rubber spatula.

6. Dust the parchment paper with a little flour mix, and transfer the dough to the lined baking sheet using a rubber spatula. Sprinkle a little more flour mix onto the dough, flour your hands, and divide the dough in half. Shape the dough into two mounded logs on the baking sheet. The dough will be sticky, so make sure your hands are really well floured. The logs should be 8 inches long by 4 inches wide by 1 inch high.

7. Using a pastry brush, brush the tops of the logs liberally with the rice milk. Then sprinkle the tops with the remaining 2 tablespoons sugar.

8. Bake in the center of the oven for 35 minutes.

9. Remove the baking sheet from the oven and reduce the temperature to 300°F. Let cool for 20 minutes, then lift the logs off the parchment paper (if they stick, use a frosting spatula to gently loosen them by sliding it gently under the bottom). Slice each log

CONTINUED

diagonally into 12 slices. I cut each log in half first, then into quarters, and then each quarter into 3 slices. I use a sharp serrated knife to do this.

10. Return the slices to the baking sheet. Bake for 20 minutes, remove from the oven, flip the cookies, and bake for 20 minutes more, or until lightly golden. Remove from the oven and transfer the biscotti to a cooling rack. They will become extra crisp once they cool.

Russian Rock Cookies

MAKES 24 2-INCH COOKIES

Spicy, exotic, buttery drop cookies—just the perfect size for dunking in a hot cup of tea or mulled apple cider.

1/2 cup dairy-free, soy-free vegetable shortening
3/4 cup granulated sugar
1 tablespoon Ener-G egg replacer mixed with
    1/4 cup rice milk
1/2 teaspoon baking soda dissolved in
    11/2 teaspoons hot water
11/4 cups Basic Gluten-Free Flour Mix (page 19)

3/4 cup golden raisins
1/4 teaspoon xanthan gum
1/4 teaspoon salt
1/2 teaspoon ground cloves
1/2 teaspoon ground nutmeg
1/2 teaspoon allspice

1. Preheat the oven to 350°F. Line two baking sheets with parchment paper.

2. In the bowl of a stand mixer fitted with the paddle attachment, cream the shortening and sugar, mixing on medium speed until light and fluffy, about 2 minutes. Add the egg replacer and baking soda mixture, and mix for 30 seconds.

3. Combine 1/4 cup of the flour mix with the raisins. Set aside.

4. Whisk together the remaining 1 cup flour mix, xanthan gum, salt, cloves, nutmeg, and allspice.

5. Add the flour mixture to the creamed batter and mix on low speed until combined, scraping down the sides of the bowl as necessary. Add the raisins and mix.

6. Drop by heaping teaspoonfuls onto the baking sheets. Bake for 12 minutes in the center of the oven, or until golden brown. Let cool on the baking sheets for 10 minutes before transferring to a cooling rack.

Dutch Cocoa Cookies

MAKES 24 2½-INCH COOKIES

My husband Adam asked me to create this recipe. He wanted a facsimile of Archway Dutch Cocoa Cookies, one of his childhood favorites. This recipe comes pretty darn close to the original, and has become a real favorite with my kids as well.

2 cups plus 2 tablespoons Basic Gluten-Free Flour Mix (page 19)
½ cup unsweetened cocoa powder
½ teaspoon plus ⅛ teaspoon xanthan gum
¾ teaspoon baking soda
1½ teaspoons cream of tartar
¼ teaspoon salt
⅓ cup vegan vanilla yogurt
1 teaspoon cider vinegar

¾ cup dairy-free, soy-free vegetable shortening
¾ cup granulated sugar
¼ cup plus 2 tablespoons firmly packed brown sugar
2 teaspoons pure vanilla extract
1½ teaspoons Ener-G egg replacer mixed with 2 tablespoons rice milk
3 tablespoons granulated sugar mixed with 1 tablespoon unsweetened cocoa powder

1. Preheat the oven to 350°F. Line two baking sheets with parchment paper.

2. Whisk together the flour mix, cocoa powder, xanthan gum, baking soda, cream of tartar, and salt.

3. In a separate bowl, whisk together the yogurt and cider vinegar.

4. In the bowl of a stand mixer fitted with the paddle attachment, combine the shortening, granulated sugar, and brown sugar, mixing on medium speed until fluffy, about 2 minutes. Add the vanilla and egg replacer. Mix for about 30 seconds.

5. Add half of the flour mixture to the creamed batter then mix on low speed. Add half of the yogurt, then add the remaining flour and yogurt, scraping down the sides of the bowl as necessary.

6. Scoop out dough by heaping tablespoonfuls and place on the baking sheets, 12 per sheet. Wet your hands with a little water and roll the dough into balls, moistening your hands again as necessary. Roll the balls in the sugar and cocoa mixture until coated on all sides. Place them back on the baking sheets. (For a flatter cookie, press gently on the shaped balls to flatten before baking.)

7. Bake in the center of the oven for 10 to 12 minutes, or until just set.

8. Let cool for 10 minutes on the baking sheet before transferring to a cooling rack.

Swedish Cardamom Cookies (Pepper Kakar)

MAKES 24 2¹/₂-INCH COOKIES

This is an old-fashioned recipe from Sweden, often baked during Christmastime. Although Swedish cuisine may be unfamiliar to most of us outside of Scandinavia, these cookies will probably taste familiar. Cardamom is the predominant spice in masala chai, the warming, aromatic tea sold by street vendors called "chai wallahs" throughout South Asia, and now also sold at Starbucks around the world, packaged as chai latte. But whether it's Starbucks, Stockholm, or India, these cookies from way up north taste like the holidays to me.

1/2 cup dairy-free, soy-free vegetable shortening
3/4 cup sugar
1¹/2 teaspoons Ener-G egg replacer mixed with
   2 tablespoons rice milk
1 tablespoon dark Karo syrup
1¹/2 cups Basic Gluten-Free Flour Mix
   (page 19)

1/4 teaspoon plus 1/8 teaspoon xanthan gum
1/8 teaspoon salt
1 teaspoon baking soda
1 teaspoon ground cinnamon
1/4 teaspoon ground cloves
1/2 teaspoon ground cardamom

1. In the bowl of a stand mixer fitted with the paddle attachment, combine the shortening, sugar, egg replacer, and Karo syrup. Beat on medium speed until light and fluffy, about 2 minutes.

2. Whisk together the flour mix, xanthan gum, salt, baking soda, cinnamon, cloves, and cardamom.

3. Add the dry ingredients to the creamed batter, and mix on low speed until combined, about 30 seconds.

4. Roll into two 5-inch logs, 2 inches in diameter.

5. Wrap in plastic wrap or waxed paper and chill for at least 1 hour, but not longer than 2 hours.

6. Preheat the oven to 325°F. Line two baking sheets with parchment paper.

7. Remove one log from the fridge and unwrap. Cut into 12 slices. The easiest way to do to this is to cut the log in half, then into quarters. Cut each quarter into 3 slices. Place the 12 cookies on one baking sheet. Repeat with the other log of cookie dough.

8. Bake in the center of the oven for 14 minutes, until set around the edges. Remove from the oven and let sit for about 10 minutes on the baking sheet before transferring to a cooling rack.

Tip ▪ If any of your slices break apart as you're cutting the log, just pinch them back together with your fingers, and flip them onto the baking sheet, pinched side down— nobody will ever know!

Quebec Maple Date Cookies

MAKES 24 2½-INCH COOKIES

This is a simple drop cookie with a delightful maple flavor. I went to college in Quebec, and these cookies transport me back to snowy winters where nothing was more warming than a freshly baked treat.

1½ cups Basic Gluten-Free Flour Mix
   (page 19)
¼ teaspoon xanthan gum
½ teaspoon double-acting baking powder
½ teaspoon baking soda
¼ teaspoon salt

½ cup chopped dates
½ cup dairy-free, soy-free vegetable
   shortening
¾ cup pure maple syrup
1 tablespoon Ener-G egg replacer mixed with
   ¼ cup rice milk

1. Preheat the oven to 350°F. Line two baking sheets with parchment paper.

2. Whisk together the flour mix, xanthan gum, baking powder, baking soda, and salt.

3. Add the dates and mix well.

4. In the bowl of a stand mixer fitted with the paddle attachment, cream the shortening on medium speed, about 1 minute. Add the maple syrup and egg replacer, and mix for about 1 minute, scraping down the sides of the bowl. It won't come together completely until you add the dry ingredients, so do not fret!

5. Add the flour mixture and mix on low speed until well incorporated, about 30 seconds.

6. Drop by heaping teaspoons onto the baking sheets and bake for 14 minutes in the center of the oven, or until lightly golden. Let cool on the baking sheets for about 10 minutes before transferring to a cooling rack.

Graham Crackers

MAKES 24 CRACKERS

These graham crackers are addictively delicious. They're great as a snack with a glass of rice milk, or wonderful made into s'mores (see variation below). This recipe also makes a wonderful pie crust.

1¼ cups Basic Gluten-Free Flour Mix (page 19)
¼ cup sorghum flour
¼ cup golden flaxseed meal
½ teaspoon xanthan gum
½ teaspoon baking soda
½ teaspoon ground cinnamon

¼ teaspoon salt
½ cup dairy-free, soy-free vegetable shortening
¼ cup plus 2 tablespoons firmly packed light brown sugar
1 tablespoon light agave nectar

1. Whisk together the flours, flaxseed meal, xanthan gum, baking soda, cinnamon, and salt. Set aside.

2. In the bowl of a stand mixer fitted with the paddle attachment, combine the shortening, light brown sugar, and agave nectar, mixing on medium speed for about 2 minutes, scraping down the sides of the bowl as necessary.

3. Add the flour mixture and beat on low speed until just combined, about 20 seconds.

4. Lay out two sheets of parchment paper. Divide the dough evenly between the two. The dough will be crumbly. Starting with one mound of dough, pat together into a disk, pressing in any loose bits, then top with another sheet of parchment paper. Roll out into a rectangular shape, 9 by 6 inches and ⅛ inch thick. Remove the top sheet of parchment paper, and use your fingers to coax the rectangle into a more uniform shape (think making pinch pots!). Top again with parchment paper, roll one more time until smooth, then remove the parchment paper and set it aside for later.

5. Using a fluted pastry wheel (or pizza cutter), divide the rectangle into three 6 by 3-inch rectangles.

6. Pressing lightly with the pastry wheel so as not to cut all the way through, score each rectangle in half lengthwise and crosswise, to form four 3 by 1 ½-inch crackers.

7. Top again with the reserved sheet of parchment paper and place on the rack in the freezer to chill for 20 minutes, or until firm.

8. Repeat with the other half of dough. You can stack them in the freezer.

9. Preheat the oven to 325°F.

10. Once the dough has chilled, remove from the freezer, remove the top sheets of parchment paper, and transfer the dough, still on the parchment paper, to a baking sheet. You can fit both on the same baking sheet, just trim off any extra parchment paper.

11. Bake for 18 minutes, or until golden brown, rotating the baking sheet halfway through. Transfer the baking sheet to a cooling rack, and let the crackers cool while still on the baking sheet. Let cool completely before breaking the crackers along the perforated lines. Store in an airtight container.

Variation ■ **S'mores:** Top one graham cracker with one piece of Enjoy Life Rice Milk Boom Choco Boom bar, then top the chocolate with a single vegan marshmallow. Microwave for about 10 seconds, or until the marshmallow puffs, then remove from the microwave and top with a second graham cracker . . . I think we have a hit!

Chocolate Rice Crispy Treats

MAKES 16 SQUARES

SunButter is used in place of marshmallow as the binder in this allergen-free version of an old favorite. In addition to being delicious, this rice crispy treat is also packed with protein and vitamin E, so you can feel indulged and virtuous, all at the same time! Dark Karo syrup contains molasses instead of high-fructose corn syrup, and thus is better in my opinion, but dark and light corn syrup are interchangeable.

1/2 cup dark Karo syrup
1/2 cup granulated sugar
1/2 cup SunButter

3 cups rice crispy cereal
1 cup dairy-free, soy-free chocolate chips

1. Grease an 8 by 8-inch pan.

2. Place the dark Karo syrup and sugar in a heavy saucepan over medium heat. Heat, stirring frequently, until the sugar dissolves and the mixture just begins to boil.

3. Remove from the heat and stir in the SunButter, mixing well until combined. Add the rice crispies and mix, working quickly. Press the mixture into the pan. Set aside.

4. Melt the chocolate chips in a microwave-safe bowl in the microwave, stirring at 30-second increments, or melt in a saucepan over low heat, stirring constantly. Spread the melted chocolate evenly over the rice crispy mixture. Let cool until the chocolate layer sets. Cut into 16 squares once cool.

Lemon-Lime Squares

MAKES 16 SQUARES

This one is an "Uh-oh, if I don't watch out, I'll eat the whole pan!" recipe. Its flavor is a cross between lemon meringue pie and key lime pie. My mother claims I'm so fond of citrus because she ate lemon meringue pie every day when she was pregnant with me. Whatever the reason, I love tart sweets, and if you do too, then this is the recipe for you. The kickin' lemon-lime pairs perfectly with the buttery shortbread crust.

Crust

1/4 cup granulated sugar

1 cup Basic Gluten-Free Flour Mix (page 19)

1/2 teaspoon xanthan gum

5 tablespoons dairy-free, soy-free vegetable shortening, chilled

Lemon-Lime Layer

4 1/2 teaspoons Ener-G egg replacer mixed with 6 tablespoons rice milk

3/4 cup granulated sugar

Juice of 1 large juicy lemon and 1 large juicy lime (you should have 1/2 cup freshly squeezed juice, so if your citrus is dry, it may take more than 2 fruits)

Zest from 1 lime

Zest from 1 lemon

1 teaspoon pure vanilla extract

1/2 teaspoon double-acting baking powder

1/8 teaspoon salt

3 tablespoons Basic Gluten-Free Flour Mix (page 19)

Confectioners' sugar, for dusting

1. Preheat the oven to 350°F. Grease an 8 by 8-inch baking pan.

2. To make the crust, combine the granulated sugar, flour mix, and xanthan gum in the bowl of a stand mixer fitted with the paddle attachment. Add the shortening and mix on medium speed until crumbly (with bits no bigger than peas).

3. Press the crust into the pan with your fingertips. Flatten with the palm of your hand.

4. Bake for 15 minutes.

5. Meanwhile, to make the lemon-lime layer, whisk the egg replacer until foamy. Add the granulated sugar, lemon juice and lime juice, lemon and lime zests, vanilla, baking powder, salt, and flour mix. Mix well.

6. Pour over the crust and bake for 25 minutes, or until set.

7. Cool completely on a cooling rack. Cover with plastic wrap and refrigerate overnight. Cut into 16 pieces, transfer to a serving plate (I find a long, thin frosting spatula works best for this), and sift the tops with confectioners' sugar. Keep stored in the fridge. If the confectioners' sugar sinks into the squares before they get eaten, just sift some more on top to refresh them! Double yum!

Fudge Brownies (page 86) and Chocolate Chunk Blondie Bars (opposite)

Chocolate Chunk Blondie Bars

MAKES 16 BARS

I was so excited when Enjoy Life came out with their new line of chocolate bars, I literally jumped for joy. I was already a huge fan of their chocolate chips, and now they've given me a whole new genre of chocolate to bake with. These chocolate chunk cookie bars are an old-fashioned picnic or school function favorite. So easy and yet sooooo good!

2 1/2 cups plus 2 tablespoons Basic Gluten-Free Flour Mix (page 19)

1/2 teaspoon plus 1/8 teaspoon xanthan gum

1 1/2 teaspoons double-acting baking powder

1/4 teaspoon salt

3/4 cup dairy-free, soy-free vegetable shortening

3/4 cup granulated sugar

1/4 cup plus 2 tablespoons firmly packed light brown sugar

2 teaspoons pure vanilla extract

1 1/2 teaspoons Ener-G egg replacer mixed with 2 tablespoons rice milk

1/4 cup plus 1 teaspoon rice milk

6 ounces (about 4 bars) Enjoy Life Rice Milk bars or Dark Chocolate Boom Choco Boom bars, chopped into centimeter-size chunks

1. Preheat the oven to 350°F. Grease a 9 by 9-inch pan.

2. Whisk together the flour mix, xanthan gum, baking powder, and salt. Set aside.

3. In the bowl of a stand mixer fitted with the paddle attachment, combine the shortening, granulated sugar, and brown sugar, beating on medium speed until light and fluffy, about 2 minutes.

4. Add the vanilla and egg replacer and mix for 20 seconds.

5. Add the flour mix in three batches, mixing on low speed, alternating with the rice milk, and beginning and ending with the flour mix.

6. Fold in the chocolate chunks.

7. Spread the batter evenly across the bottom of the baking pan.

8. Bake in the center of the oven for 35 minutes, or until lightly golden, rotating the pan halfway through.

9. Remove from the oven and let cool in the pan on a cooling rack for about 15 minutes. Cut into 16 squares. Let cool.

Fudge Brownies

MAKES 16 BROWNIES

Up until I created this recipe, allergen-free, gluten-free brownies were a bit like the Holy Grail. I kept searching, but to no avail. I worked on my own recipe, but making brownies without dairy, soy, gluten, and, most of all, eggs is not easy! Granted, there were recipes out there that called themselves brownies, but they were really just mini cupcakes. A chewy, moist brownie with a nice crusty, glossy top remained elusive. Until now, that is. Yup, that's right, after years of trying, I've finally baked it—an honest-to-goodness allergen-free, gluten-free, vegan tray of real brownies. Go ahead, I dare you, try eating just one.

6 ounces unsweetened chocolate, chopped into centimeter-size pieces (a serrated knife works best for this)

1/2 cup dairy-free, soy-free vegetable shortening

2 cups granulated sugar

2 (4- to 5-ounce) jars prune purée or apple plum purée (baby food)

1 tablespoon pure vanilla extract

13/4 cups plus 2 tablespoons Basic Gluten-Free Flour Mix (page 19)

1/2 teaspoon xanthan gum

1 tablespoon double-acting baking powder

1 1/2 cups dairy-free, soy-free chocolate chips

1. Preheat the oven to 325°F. Grease a 9 by 9-inch baking pan, then sprinkle with a little gluten-free flour mix, tapping out any extra.

2. Combine the unsweetened chocolate and shortening in a microwave-safe bowl and melt in the microwave, stopping to check and stir every 30 seconds. (Alternatively, you can melt the chocolate and shortening in a double boiler.) Once melted, stir in the sugar and prune purée. Mix well, add the vanilla, and beat until smooth.

3. Whisk together the flour mix, xanthan gum, and baking powder. Add to the chocolate mixture in three batches, stirring well after each addition. Beat until smooth. Fold in the chocolate chips.

4. Spread the batter in the prepared pan, smoothing down the top with the back of a rubber spatula or large spoon. Bake in the center of the oven for 55 minutes, rotating the pan halfway through. Bake until the top looks glossy and the brownie is just beginning to pull away from the sides of the pan.

5. Let the brownies cool completely in the pan, then cut into squares. Remove from the pan and enjoy. Store in an airtight container.

Coconut Chip Bars

MAKES 16 BARS

Often called "dream bars," these double-layered bar cookies have a crunchy graham cracker base and a chewy, caramelized top. My friend Ben Duke says, "The only problem with these cookies is that there aren't more of them!"

1 recipe Graham Crackers (page 80)
1 tablespoon Ener-G egg replacer mixed with
    1/4 cup rice milk
1 cup firmly packed light brown sugar
2 tablespoons Basic Gluten-Free Flour Mix
    (page 19)

1/2 teaspoon double-acting baking powder
11/2 cups unsweetened coconut flakes
1 cup dairy-free, soy-free chocolate chips

1. Follow the Graham Crackers recipe (page 80) up to step 3. Grease a 9 by 9-inch baking pan and sprinkle with a little gluten-free flour mix. Press the crust into the pan with your fingertips. Flatten with the palm of your hand, and prick about 9 times with a fork. Chill in the freezer for 20 minutes, or until firm.

2. Preheat the oven to 350°F.

3. Bake the crust in the center of the oven for 10 minutes.

4. Meanwhile, whisk the egg replacer until foamy. Add the light brown sugar, flour mix, and baking powder. Mix well. Add the coconut flakes and chocolate chips and combine.

5. Spread the topping evenly over the crust, and bake for another 20 minutes, or until golden.

6. Cool completely on a cooling rack. Cut into 16 squares. Store in the fridge.

Red Velvet Cake with Velvet Frosting (page 109)

5

CAKES

Cake is defined in the *Encyclopedia Brittanica* as "In general, any of a variety of breads, shortened or unshortened, usually shaped by the tin in which it is baked; more specifically, a sweetened bread, often rich or delicate." But to me, cake also means birthday party, family gathering, milestone, pick-me-up, pick-you-up, congratulations, you're on vacation, you deserve a break today, special breakfast, dessert, afternoon tea, or late night snack. As you've probably guessed, we Pascals are crazy for cake.

I have offered quite a few options for cupcakes in this chapter, since they are the most popular cake these days. Like cookies, they are self-contained little treats that are easy to transport, and are just the perfect size. Another thing that's great about cupcakes for those with food allergies is that they freeze really well, so whenever a birthday party or other celebratory occasion pops up at which there will be off-limits treats, you or your child can rest assured that you have your own far superior allergen-free delight. Don't be surprised if the other partygoers look at you with envy and ask, "Where did you get that delicious-looking cupcake?" If you're feeling particularly generous, you could always bring a batch of them to share with the others, and watch their enchantment when they discover it's allergen-free.

This chapter also covers traditional layer cakes and teacakes, many of which double well as breakfast. There is something here for every cake lover, whether you want rich and chocolaty, classic, free of refined sugar, low-fat, or just plain decadent. Go ahead, have your cake and eat it too!

Chocolate Cupcakes with Chocolate Buttercream Frosting

MAKES 12 CUPCAKES

So simple, yet so perfect. These cupcakes are topped with a chocolate buttercream frosting made with no butter, no cream—but it's rich, chocolaty, and creamy nonetheless! This frosting will frost 12 cupcakes if you're piping it, more if you're just spreading the frosting. If you have leftover frosting, it will keep for weeks tightly covered in the fridge. Just let it come to room temperature and whip it up again. For added panache, dress these cupcakes up with sprinkles for kids' birthday parties, or top them with Rice Milk Chocolate Ganache (page 104).

1 cup rice milk

1 teaspoon cider vinegar

1 cup Basic Gluten-Free Flour Mix (page 19)

1/2 cup unsweetened cocoa powder

1/4 teaspoon plus 1/8 teaspoon xanthan gum

3/4 teaspoon baking soda

1/2 teaspoon double-acting baking powder

1/4 teaspoon salt

3/4 cup granulated sugar

1/3 cup canola oil

11/2 teaspoons pure vanilla extract

1 recipe Chocolate Buttercream Frosting
(recipe follows)

1. Preheat the oven to 350°F. Line a muffin pan with 12 liners.

2. Combine the rice milk and cider vinegar, and set aside.

3. Whisk together the flour mix, cocoa powder, xanthan gum, baking soda, baking powder, and salt. Thoroughly whisk out any lumps of cocoa. Set aside.

4. In the bowl of a stand mixer fitted with the paddle attachment, combine the rice milk mixture with the sugar, canola oil, and vanilla. Beat on medium speed until light and foamy, about 1 minute.

5. Using a sifter, sift in the flour mixture in three batches, mixing on low speed. Mix until smooth, about 30 seconds.

6. Fill the muffin liners two-thirds full.

7. Bake in the center of the oven for 18 minutes, rotating the pan halfway through. Bake until a skewer inserted into the center of a cupcake comes out clean. Let the cupcakes cool in the pan for 5 minutes, then transfer to a cooling rack to cool completely before frosting.

Chocolate Buttercream Frosting ■ MAKES ENOUGH FOR 12 CUPCAKES (OR 2 8-INCH CAKES)

6 tablespoons dairy-free, soy-free
    vegetable shortening
2 2/3 cups confectioners' sugar
1/2 cup unsweetened cocoa powder

1/3 cup plus 1 tablespoon rice milk
1/2 teaspoon vanilla extract
Pinch of salt

1. In the bowl of a stand mixer fitted with the paddle attachment, beat the shortening on medium speed until light and fluffy, about 2 minutes.

2. In a separate bowl, whisk together the confectioners' sugar and cocoa powder, being sure to work out any lumps.

3. Combine the sugar mixture with the shortening, alternating with the rice milk. Add the vanilla and salt. Beat until smooth and fluffy, about 5 minutes. You can either pipe the frosting or spread it with a butter knife or frosting spatula, creating pretty swirls.

Tip ■ These rich chocolate cupcakes are also delicious with Vanilla Frosting (page 93) or SunButter Buttercream (page 102).

Vanilla Cupcakes with Vanilla Frosting

MAKES 12 CUPCAKES

The perfect birthday cupcake, these vanilla beauties can be decorated any way you like. Top them with confetti, decorating sugar, sugared violets, edible flowers . . . the possibilities are endless. My husband says they taste like a vegan Twinkie. I take that as a compliment.

2 cups Basic Gluten-Free Flour Mix (page 19)
1/2 teaspoon xanthan gum
1 teaspoon double-acting baking powder
1 teaspoon baking soda
1 teaspoon salt
1 cup rice milk
1 teaspoon cider vinegar

1/2 cup dairy-free, soy-free vegetable shortening
1 cup granulated sugar
1 tablespoon Ener-G egg replacer mixed with 1/4 cup rice milk
11/2 teaspoons pure vanilla extract
1 recipe Vanilla Frosting (recipe follows)

1. Preheat the oven to 350°F. Line a muffin pan with 12 liners.

2. Whisk together the flour mix, xanthan gum, baking powder, baking soda, and salt. Set aside.

3. Combine the rice milk and cider vinegar. Set aside.

4. In the bowl of a stand mixer fitted with the paddle attachment, combine the shortening, sugar, egg replacer, and vanilla. Beat on medium speed until light and fluffy, about 2 minutes. Sift in the flour mixture in three batches, alternating with the rice milk, and beginning and ending with the flour mixture. Beat until smooth, scraping down the sides of the bowl as necessary, about 30 seconds.

5. Fill the liners three-fourths full with batter. Smooth the tops with a butter knife or frosting spatula.

6. Bake in the center of the oven for about 22 minutes, rotating the pan halfway through. Bake until golden and a skewer inserted into the center of a cupcake comes out clean. Transfer the cupcakes to a cooling rack and let cool completely before frosting and decorating as you wish.

Vanilla Frosting ∎ MAKES ENOUGH FOR 12 CUPCAKES (OR 2 8-INCH CAKES)

1 cup dairy-free, soy-free vegetable
   shortening
Pinch of salt

3 cups confectioners' sugar
1/4 cup rice milk
1/2 teaspoon pure vanilla extract

1. In the bowl of a stand mixer fitted with the paddle attachment, cream the shortening and salt on medium speed for about 1 minute.

2. Add the confectioners' sugar, rice milk, and vanilla. Beat until smooth and fluffy, about 5 minutes. You can either pipe the frosting or spread it with a butter knife or frosting spatula, creating pretty swirls.

Tip ∎ If you're into making cupcakes, invest in a mechanical pastry bag. Williams-Sonoma makes a great one, and it will make piping frosting an easy dream. No more fussing with messy pastry bags—just fill and press. I truly love mine, and I don't use the word *love* lightly.

Carrot Ginger Cupcakes with Orange Buttercream Frosting

MAKES 12 CUPCAKES

Of all the cupcakes in this book, these are my favorite. When I baked up a dozen, I personally consumed nine out of twelve. I even ate the one I had set aside for my husband. Yup, it's true. They're that good.

1½ cups Basic Gluten-Free Flour Mix (page 19)

¼ teaspoon plus ⅛ teaspoon xanthan gum

1 teaspoon double-acting baking powder

½ teaspoon baking soda

½ teaspoon salt

½ teaspoon ground cinnamon

2¼ teaspoons Ener-G egg replacer mixed with 3 tablespoons orange juice

3 tablespoons plain or vanilla vegan yogurt

½ teaspoon pure vanilla extract

1 cup granulated sugar

¾ cup canola oil

1 teaspoon grated fresh ginger

1¼ cups finely shredded carrots

1 recipe Orange Buttercream Frosting (recipe follows)

1. Preheat the oven to 350°F. Line a muffin pan with 12 liners.

2. Whisk together the flour mix, xanthan gum, baking powder, baking soda, salt, and cinnamon in a large bowl. Set aside.

3. Combine the egg replacer, vegan yogurt, vanilla, sugar, canola oil, and fresh ginger, stirring well, about 1 minute. Add the carrots and mix until combined.

4. Add the flour mixture, folding it into the carrot mixture, until completely combined.

5. Fill the muffin liners about three-fourths full of batter.

6. Bake in the center of the oven for 24 minutes, rotating the pan halfway through. Bake until a skewer inserted into the center of a cupcake comes out clean. Transfer the cupcakes to a cooling rack and let cool completely before frosting.

Orange Buttercream Frosting ■ MAKES ENOUGH FOR 12 CUPCAKES (OR 2 8-INCH CAKES)

1 cup dairy-free, soy-free vegetable shortening
3 cups confectioners' sugar
1/4 cup orange juice

2 teaspoons orange zest
Pinch of salt

1. In the bowl of a stand mixer fitted with the paddle attachment, cream the shortening on medium speed, about 2 minutes.

2. Add the confectioners' sugar in three batches, mixing after each addition.

3. Add the orange juice, orange zest, and salt.

4. Beat on medium speed until light and fluffy, about 5 minutes. You can either pipe the frosting or spread it with a butter knife or frosting spatula, creating pretty swirls.

Tip ■ To make as a layer cake, double the recipe and use 2 8-inch round cake pans. Bake for 35 to 40 minutes.

Coconut Cupcakes

MAKES 12 CUPCAKES

These look like Hostess Sno Balls but are much healthier. They taste sublime, and are so very, very pretty.

1¹/2 cups Basic Gluten-Free Flour Mix
    (page 19)
¹/4 teaspoon plus ¹/8 teaspoon xanthan gum
³/4 teaspoon double-acting baking powder
³/4 teaspoon baking soda
¹/2 teaspoon salt
¹/2 cup plain or vanilla vegan yogurt
¹/2 cup coconut milk
1¹/2 teaspoons freshly squeezed lemon juice

¹/4 cup coconut oil, at room temperature
³/4 cup granulated sugar
2¹/4 teaspoons egg replacer mixed with
    3 tablespoons rice milk
1 teaspoon pure vanilla extract
1 teaspoon coconut extract/flavor
¹/2 cup unsweetened shredded coconut
1 recipe Coconut Frosting (recipe follows)
1¹/2 cups unsweetened coconut flakes

1. Preheat the oven to 350°F. Line a muffin pan with 12 liners.

2. Whisk together the flour mix, xanthan gum, baking powder, baking soda, and salt. Set aside.

3. Combine the vegan yogurt, coconut milk, and lemon juice. Set aside.

4. In the bowl of a stand mixer fitted with the paddle attachment, combine the coconut oil, sugar, egg replacer, vanilla, and coconut extract. Beat for about 2 minutes on medium speed. Sift in the flour mixture in three batches, alternating with the yogurt/coconut milk mixture, and beginning and ending with the flour mixture. Beat until smooth, about 30 seconds, scraping down the sides of the bowl as necessary. Fold in the shredded coconut.

5. Fill the liners three-fourths full with batter. Smooth the tops of the cupcakes with a butter knife or frosting spatula.

6. Bake in the center of the oven for about 22 minutes, rotating the pan halfway through. Bake until golden and a skewer inserted into the center of a cupcake comes out clean. Transfer the cupcakes to a cooling rack and let cool completely before frosting.

7. To frost the cupcakes, cover the tops of the cupcakes liberally with frosting, then roll gently in the flaked coconut.

Coconut Frosting ■ MAKES ENOUGH FOR 12 CUPCAKES (OR 2 8-INCH CAKES)

3/4 cup dairy-free, soy-free vegetable
   shortening
Pinch of salt
21/4 cups confectioners' sugar

3 tablespoons rice milk
1/2 teaspoon coconut extract/flavor
1/2 teaspoon pure vanilla extract

1. In the bowl of a stand mixer fitted with the paddle attachment, cream the shortening and salt on medium speed for about 2 minutes.

2. Add the confectioners' sugar in three batches, beating after each addition.

3. Add the rice milk, coconut extract, and vanilla. Beat until light and fluffy, about 5 minutes.

4. Spread the frosting with a butter knife or frosting spatula, mounding over the tops of the cupcakes.

Vanilla Cupcakes with Vanilla Frosting (page 92), Chocolate Chip Cupcakes with Chocolate Chip Frosting (opposite), and Carrot Ginger Cupcakes with Orange Buttercream Frosting (page 94)

Chocolate Chip Cupcakes with Chocolate Chip Frosting

MAKES 12 CUPCAKES

These could just as easily be called "Allergen-Free Heaven." Need I say more?

1/2 cup rice milk
1/2 teaspoon cider vinegar
1 1/2 cups plus 1 1/2 tablespoons Basic Gluten-Free Flour Mix (page 19)
1/2 teaspoon xanthan gum
1 teaspoon double-acting baking powder
1/2 teaspoon baking soda
1/2 teaspoon salt

1/2 cup dairy-free, soy-free vegetable shortening
1 cup plus 2 tablespoons granulated sugar
1 tablespoon Ener-G egg replacer mixed with 1/4 cup rice milk
1/2 teaspoon pure vanilla extract
1 cup dairy-free, soy-free chocolate chips
1 recipe Chocolate Chip Frosting (recipe follows)

1. Preheat the oven to 350°F. Line a muffin pan with 12 liners.

2. Combine the rice milk and cider vinegar and set aside.

3. Whisk together the flour mix, xanthan gum, baking powder, baking soda, and salt.

4. In the bowl of a stand mixer fitted with the paddle attachment, combine the shortening, sugar, egg replacer, and vanilla. Beat on medium speed until light and fluffy, about 2 minutes. Sift in the flour mixture in three batches, alternating with the rice milk mixture, and beginning and ending with the flour mixture. Beat until smooth, about 30 seconds, scraping down the sides of the bowl as necessary. Fold in the chocolate chips.

5. Fill liners three-fourths full with batter. Smooth the tops of the cupcakes with a butter knife or frosting spatula.

6. Bake in the center of the oven for 24 minutes, rotating the pan halfway through. Bake until a skewer inserted into the center of a cupcake comes out clean. Transfer the cupcakes to a cooling rack and let cool completely before frosting.

CONTINUED

Chocolate Chip Frosting ■ MAKES ENOUGH FOR 12 CUPCAKES (OR 2 8-INCH CAKES)

3/4 cup dairy-free, soy-free vegetable shortening
Pinch of salt
2 1/4 cups confectioners' sugar

3 tablespoons rice milk
1/2 teaspoon pure vanilla extract
1 cup dairy-free, soy-free chocolate chips

1. In the bowl of a stand mixer fitted with the paddle attachment, cream the shortening and salt on medium speed for about 2 minutes.

2. Add the confectioners' sugar in three batches, beating after each addition.

3. Add the rice milk and vanilla. Beat until light and fluffy, about 5 minutes. Fold in the chocolate chips. Spread the frosting with a butter knife or frosting spatula, mounding over the tops of the cupcakes.

Tip ■ Cupcakes keep well for at least 3 days when stored covered in the fridge. They also freeze well, so pop them in the freezer, then remove and let come to room temperature for a little cake anytime.

SunButter Cupcakes with SunButter Buttercream

MAKES 12 CUPCAKES

SunButter is truly a gift from the gods for kids with peanut and tree nut allergies. These cupcakes are delicious and nutritious. Top them with SunButter Buttercream or with Rice Milk Chocolate Ganache for a refined sugar–free treat. Or go for broke, and pipe the tops with SunButter Buttercream, and then drizzle with Rice Milk Chocolate Ganache!

1/2 cup plus 2 tablespoons rice milk

2 teaspoons cider vinegar

1/2 cup crunchy SunButter

1/3 cup canola oil

2/3 cup Sucanat or firmly packed brown sugar

11/2 teaspoons pure vanilla extract

1 tablespoon flaxseed meal mixed with
   3 tablespoons hot water ("flax egg")

11/4 cups Basic Gluten-Free Flour Mix (page 19)

1/4 teaspoon plus 1/8 teaspoon xanthan gum

1 teaspoon double-acting baking powder

1/2 teaspoon baking soda

1/4 teaspoon salt

1 recipe SunButter Buttercream (recipe
   follows) and/or Rice Milk Chocolate
   Ganache (page 104)

1. Preheat the oven to 350°F. Line a muffin pan with 12 muffin liners.

2. Combine the rice milk and cider vinegar. Set aside.

3. In the bowl of a stand mixer fitted with the paddle attachment, beat the crunchy SunButter on medium speed for about 2 minutes.

4. Add the canola oil, Sucanat, and vanilla and beat for about 3 minutes more. Add the flax egg and mix until thoroughly combined.

5. Whisk together the flour mix, xanthan gum, baking powder, baking soda, and salt.

6. Sift the flour mix into the SunButter mixture in three batches, alternating with the rice milk mixture, beginning and ending with the flour mixture, and mixing until combined, about 30 seconds.

7. Fill the liners half full, smooth the tops a bit, and bake in the center of the oven for 22 minutes, or until a rich golden color, rotating the pan halfway through. Remove from the oven and let cool in the pan for 5 minutes before transferring to a cooling rack to finish cooling completely before frosting. Frost with SunButter Buttercream.

CONTINUED

SunButter Buttercream ■ MAKES ENOUGH TO FROST 12 CUPCAKES (OR 2 8-INCH CAKES)

1/4 cup plus 2 tablespoons dairy-free, soy-free vegetable shortening

1/3 cup smooth SunButter

1 1/2 teaspoons pure vanilla extract

1 1/4 cups confectioners' sugar

2 tablespoons rice milk

1. In the bowl of a stand mixer fitted with the paddle attachment, cream the shortening, SunButter, and vanilla on medium speed for about 2 minutes.

2. Add the confectioners' sugar, mix (it will be crumbly), then add the rice milk. Beat on medium speed for 5 minutes, or until fluffy and smooth. You can either pipe the frosting or spread it with a butter knife or frosting spatula, creating pretty swirls.

Chocolate Maple Cupcakes with Rice Milk Chocolate Ganache

MAKES 12 CUPCAKES

Maple syrup is a great way to sweeten chocolate treats in place of refined sugar. I prefer to use Grade B maple syrup, which is richer in flavor, higher in nutrients, but lighter on the wallet than Grade A.

2/3 cup rice milk

1 teaspoon cider vinegar

1 cup Basic Gluten-Free Flour Mix (page 19)

1/2 cup unsweetened cocoa powder

1/4 teaspoon plus 1/8 teaspoon xanthan gum

3/4 teaspoon baking soda

1/2 teaspoon double-acting baking powder

1/4 teaspoon salt

1/2 cup dairy-free, soy-free vegetable shortening

2/3 cup maple syrup

11/2 teaspoons pure vanilla extract

1 recipe Rice Milk Chocolate Ganache (recipe follows)

1. Preheat the oven to 350°F. Line a muffin pan with 12 liners.

2. Combine the rice milk and cider vinegar. Set aside.

3. Whisk together the flour mix, cocoa powder, xanthan gum, baking soda, baking powder, and salt.

4. In the bowl of a stand mixer fitted with the paddle attachment, cream the shortening on medium speed for about 1 minute. Add the maple syrup and vanilla, and beat for about 3 minutes, or until combined. (Don't worry if it's mottled; it all comes together once you add the dry ingredients.)

5. Sift in the dry ingredients in three batches, alternating with the rice milk mixture, and beginning and ending with the dry ingredients. Beat until smooth, about 30 seconds, scraping down the sides of the bowl as necessary. Fill the liners about half full.

6. Bake in the center of the oven for about 18 minutes, rotating the pan halfway through. Bake until a skewer inserted into the center of a cupcake comes out clean.

7. Transfer the cupcakes to a cooling rack and let cool completely before topping with the ganache. For easy cleanup, line a baking sheet with waxed paper or parchment paper and transfer the cupcakes to the baking sheet. I usually spread 1 teaspoon on each cupcake, then go back and top each with a second teaspoon, for a nice glossy, even layer.

CONTINUED

Rice Milk Chocolate Ganache ■ MAKES ENOUGH TO GLAZE 12 CUPCAKES

4 Enjoy Life Rice Milk Boom Choco Boom bars (about 6 ounces total), or 1 cup dairy-free, soy-free chocolate chips

1/4 cup rice milk
2 tablespoons maple syrup or agave nectar
Pinch of salt

1. Chop the chocolate bars into small pieces using a serrated knife.

2. Bring the rice milk to a simmer in a small saucepan over medium-high heat. Remove the pan from the heat and stir in the chopped chocolate, maple syrup, and salt.

3. Whisk until smooth, about 1 minute. Let cool to room temperature before spreading or drizzling on cupcakes. If you want the ganache to set faster, place the glazed cupcakes in the fridge.

Golden Agave Cupcakes

MAKES 12 CUPCAKES

These lightly floral, agave-sweetened gems are a multipurpose cupcake. Pair them with any frosting you like.

2/3 cup rice milk

1 teaspoon cider vinegar

1 1/2 cups Basic Gluten-Free Flour Mix (page 19)

1/4 teaspoon plus 1/8 teaspoon xanthan gum

3/4 teaspoon baking soda

1/2 teaspoon double-acting baking powder

1/4 teaspoon salt

1/2 cup dairy-free, soy-free vegetable shortening

2/3 cup agave nectar

1 1/2 teaspoons pure vanilla extract

1. Preheat the oven to 350°F. Line a muffin pan with 12 liners.

2. Combine the rice milk and cider vinegar. Set aside.

3. Whisk together the flour mix, xanthan gum, baking soda, baking powder, and salt.

4. In the bowl of a stand mixer fitted with the paddle attachment, cream the shortening on medium speed for about 1 minute. Add the agave nectar and vanilla and beat for 2 minutes more, or until combined.

5. Sift in the dry ingredients in three batches, alternating with the rice milk mixture, beginning and ending with the dry ingredients. Beat until smooth, about 30 seconds, scraping down the sides of the bowl as necessary. Fill the liners about half full.

6. Bake in the center of the oven for 18 minutes, or until a lovely golden color, rotating the pan halfway through.

7. Transfer the cupcakes to a cooling rack and let cool completely before frosting.

Chocolate Layer Cake with Dark Chocolate Frosting

MAKES 1 8-INCH LAYER CAKE

This is the ultimate chocolate birthday cake. It keeps well for days, covered or wrapped in the fridge, staying moist and rich. My friend Erika, who can eat wheat, dairy, and eggs, marveled at how delicious this cake is; her husband (who never eats frosting) loved this one so much he ate all the frosting first, then ate the cake part. When people who have no dietary restrictions eat my recipes simply because they desire them, not out of necessity, then I know I've done my job.

2¹/₂ cups Basic Gluten-Free Flour Mix (page 19)

1¹/₄ cups unsweetened cocoa powder

1 teaspoon xanthan gum

2¹/₂ cups granulated sugar

2¹/₂ teaspoons baking soda

1¹/₄ teaspoons double-acting baking powder

1¹/₄ teaspoons salt

1 tablespoon Ener-G egg replacer mixed with ¹/₄ cup rice milk

1¹/₄ cups rice milk

¹/₂ cup plus 2 tablespoons canola oil

1¹/₂ teaspoons pure vanilla extract

1¹/₄ cups warm water

1 recipe Dark Chocolate Frosting (recipe follows)

1. Preheat the oven to 350°F. Grease two 8-inch round cake pans, line with cutout parchment paper, grease again, and dust with a little cocoa powder.

2. In the bowl of a stand mixer fitted with the paddle attachment, whisk together the flour mix, cocoa powder, xanthan gum, sugar, baking soda, baking powder, and salt.

3. Add the egg replacer, rice milk, canola oil, vanilla, and warm water and beat on medium-low speed until smooth, about 3 minutes, scraping down the sides of the bowl as necessary.

4. Divide the batter evenly between the two pans.

5. Bake in the center of the oven for about 45 minutes, rotating the pans halfway through. Bake until the cake is pulling away slightly from the sides of the pans and a skewer inserted into the center of the cake comes out clean.

6. Let cool in the pans on a cooling rack for 30 minutes. Cover the cake pan with a large plate, flip, peel off the parchment paper, and flip the cake back onto the rack, right side up, to cool completely. Repeat with the other cake.

7. Once the cakes have cooled completely, you may use a serrated knife to trim the tops to make them level. Frost with Dark Chocolate Frosting (or Vanilla Frosting, page 93, or Chocolate Buttercream Frosting, page 91). Once the frosting sets, store covered.

Dark Chocolate Frosting ■ MAKES ENOUGH TO FROST 1 8-INCH LAYER CAKE

1 (10-ounce) bag Enjoy Life semisweet
    chocolate chips (1 1/2 cups)
1/4 cup unsweetened cocoa powder
1/4 cup boiling water

1 cup dairy-free, soy-free vegetable
    shortening
1/4 cup confectioners' sugar
Pinch of salt
1 tablespoon rice milk

1. Place the chocolate chips in a microwave-safe bowl. Melt in the microwave, stopping to stir every 30 seconds. It will take about 2 minutes to melt them. Stir until smooth, about 1 minute. Let cool to room temperature.

2. Combine the cocoa powder and boiling water in a small bowl, stirring until smooth and the cocoa has dissolved completely.

3. In the bowl of a stand mixer fitted with the paddle attachment, combine the shortening, confectioners' sugar, salt, and rice milk, beating on medium speed for about 3 minutes, or until light and fluffy.

4. Add the melted chocolate and beat on low speed for 2 minutes, scraping down the sides of the bowl as necessary. Add the cocoa mixture, and beat for about 1 more minute, or until combined.

Note ■ This frosting sets after a few hours, hardening into a shell. I like it this way, but if you prefer a softer frosting, add a little more boiling water or shortening. The frosting will be slightly less chocolaty, but it will be soft.

Classic Yellow Cake

MAKES 1 8-INCH LAYER CAKE

Classic, timeless, and so versatile. Dress this lovely up with Chocolate Buttercream Frosting (page 91), Dark Chocolate Frosting (page 107), or Vanilla Frosting (page 93), as suits your mood.

3 cups Basic Gluten-Free Flour Mix (page 19)
3/4 teaspoon xanthan gum
1 1/2 teaspoons double-acting baking powder
1 1/2 teaspoons baking soda
1 teaspoon salt
1 1/2 cups plain or vanilla vegan yogurt
1 tablespoon freshly squeezed lemon juice

3/4 cup dairy-free, soy-free vegetable shortening, at room temperature
1 1/2 cups granulated sugar
4 1/2 teaspoons Ener-G egg replacer mixed with 6 tablespoons rice milk
1 tablespoon pure vanilla extract
1 recipe Chocolate Buttercream Frosting (page 91) or other frosting of choice

1. Preheat the oven to 350°F. Grease two 8-inch round cake pans, line with cutout parchment paper, grease again, and dust with a little flour mix.

2. Whisk together the flour mix, xanthan gum, baking powder, baking soda, and salt. Set aside.

3. Combine the vegan yogurt and lemon juice. Set aside.

4. In the bowl of a stand mixer fitted with the paddle attachment, cream the shortening on medium speed for about 1 minute, then add the sugar, egg replacer, and vanilla. Beat on medium speed until light and fluffy, about 2 minutes. Add the flour mixture in three batches, alternating with the yogurt, beginning and ending with the flour mixture. Beat until smooth, about 30 seconds, scraping down the sides of the bowl as necessary.

5. Divide the batter evenly between the pans, smoothing down the surface with a frosting spatula.

6. Bake in the center of the oven for about 33 minutes, or until golden and a skewer inserted into the center of a cake comes out clean. Rotate the pans halfway through the baking time. Transfer the pans to a cooling rack. Let cool in the pans for 30 minutes.

7. Cover the cake pan with a large plate, flip, peel off the parchment paper, and flip the cake back onto the rack, right side up, to cool completely. Repeat with the other cake.

8. Once the cakes have cooled completely, you may use a serrated knife to trim the tops to make them level, if necessary. Frost. Once the frosting has set, store covered.

Tip ■ For a deeper yellow hue, add 1 teaspoon yellow food coloring before you add the flour mixture. Try Seelect Natural Yellow Food Coloring, which is made with turmeric. See Resources, page 177.

Red Velvet Cake with Velvet Frosting

MAKES 1 8-INCH LAYER CAKE

My whole family goes crazy for red velvet cake. It's so gorgeous and festive and sounds so luxe. This old-fashioned Southern favorite can be made even healthier by using Seelect Natural Food Coloring, which I order online (see Resources, page 177). That way, you can let them eat cake without the slightest tinge of guilt.

2³/₄ cups Basic Gluten-Free Flour Mix
   (page 19)
¹/₄ cup unsweetened cocoa powder
³/₄ teaspoon xanthan gum
1¹/₂ teaspoons double-acting baking powder
1¹/₂ teaspoons baking soda
1¹/₂ teaspoons salt
1¹/₂ cups rice milk
1¹/₂ teaspoons cider vinegar

³/₄ cup dairy-free, soy-free vegetable
   shortening
1¹/₂ cups granulated sugar
4¹/₂ teaspoons Ener-G egg replacer mixed
   with 6 tablespoons rice milk
1 teaspoon pure vanilla extract
1 (1-ounce) bottle red food coloring
1 recipe Velvet Frosting (recipe follows)

1. Preheat the oven to 350°F. Grease two 8-inch round cake pans, line with cutout parchment paper, grease again, and dust with a little cocoa powder.

2. Whisk together the flour mix, cocoa powder, xanthan gum, baking powder, baking soda, and salt. Set aside.

3. Combine the rice milk and cider vinegar. Set aside.

4. In the bowl of a stand mixer fitted with the paddle attachment, combine the shortening, sugar, egg replacer, and vanilla. Beat on medium speed until light and fluffy, about 2 minutes. Add the food coloring and mix until combined, scraping down the sides of the bowl as necessary. Sift in the flour mixture in three batches, alternating with the rice milk mixture, and beginning and ending with the flour mixture. Beat until smooth, about 30 seconds, scraping down the sides of the bowl as necessary.

5. Divide the batter between the two pans, and smooth down the surface using a frosting spatula.

6. Bake in the center of the oven for about 35 minutes, or until the cake is beginning to pull away from the sides of the pan and a skewer inserted into the center comes out clean. Rotate the pans halfway through the baking time.

7. Let cool in the pans on a cooling rack for 30 minutes. Cover the cake pan with a large plate, flip, peel off the parchment paper, and flip the cake back onto the rack, right side up, to cool completely. Repeat with the other cake.

CONTINUED

8. Once the cakes have cooled completely, you may use a serrated knife to trim the tops to make them level. Frost with Velvet Frosting. Once the frosting has set, store covered at room temperature. This cake is even better on days two and three!

Velvet Frosting ■ MAKES ENOUGH TO FROST 1 8-INCH LAYER CAKE

1 cup dairy-free, soy-free vegetable shortening
Pinch of salt
3 cups confectioners' sugar

3 tablespoons rice milk
1 tablespoon freshly squeezed lemon juice
1 teaspoon pure vanilla extract

1. In the bowl of a stand mixer fitted with the paddle attachment, cream the shortening and salt on medium speed for 1 minute.

2. Add the confectioners' sugar in three batches, beating after each addition.

3. Add the rice milk, lemon juice, and vanilla. Beat on medium speed until smooth, creamy, and fluffy, about 5 minutes.

Strawberry Shortcake with Vegan Whipped Topping

MAKES 1 8-INCH LAYER CAKE

Old-fashioned shortcake is made with biscuit dough, not cake batter. This makes a great fresh dessert or a fancy weekend breakfast. You eat it warm, straight from the oven! And the Vegan Whipped Topping is an extra-special treat. I was unable to find a dairy-free, soy-free whipped topping, so I whipped up my own! Use it anywhere you'd use whipped cream.

4 cups fresh strawberries

3 tablespoons granulated sugar

2 cups Basic Gluten-Free Flour Mix (page 19)

1/2 teaspoon xanthan gum

4 teaspoons double-acting baking powder

1/2 teaspoon salt

Pinch of ground nutmeg

1/2 cup dairy-free, soy-free vegetable shortening

3/4 cup plus 2 tablespoons rice milk

1 recipe Vegan Whipped Topping (recipe follows)

1. Preheat the oven to 425°F. Line a baking sheet with parchment paper.

2. Select 6 of the prettiest strawberries and set aside. Gently crush the remaining strawberries and toss with 2 tablespoons of the sugar. Set aside.

3. Whisk together the flour mix, xanthan gum, baking powder, salt, remaining 1 tablespoon sugar, and nutmeg in a large bowl. Add 1/4 cup of the vegetable shortening and cut in with a pastry blender, two knives, or just use your fingers. Make a well in the center and pour in 3/4 cup of the rice milk. Stir with a wooden spoon, scraping up any crumbs from the bottom of the bowl. Drizzle the remaining 2 tablespoons rice milk into the dough and work in, until the dough holds together.

4. Turn out the dough onto a floured board and divide in half. Pat or roll out into two 8-inch rounds. Slide a frosting spatula under each round to loosen them from the board. Carefully transfer the first round to the parchment-lined baking sheet. Warm 2 tablespoons of the remaining shortening until soft enough to spread easily (I give it 30 seconds in the microwave) and brush over the top of the first round. Top with the second round and bake in the center of the oven for 12 minutes, or until lightly golden.

5. Remove from the oven and use a frosting spatula to gently separate the layers, sliding it between them all the way around. Split the two layers. Transfer the bottom layer to a serving plate or cake stand.

6. Spread the bottom layer of the shortcake with the remaining 2 tablespoons of shortening. Warm the crushed berries slightly. Spoon half over the bottom layer of shortcake, cover with the top layer, and spoon the remaining berries over the top. Line the outer rim of the cake with the reserved whole strawberries. Fill the center with the Vegan Whipped Topping (I pipe it on in a swirling pattern, but you could just as easily spoon it). This shortcake is best eaten immediately.

Vegan Whipped Topping ■ MAKES 1¹/₂ CUPS

2 tablespoons cornstarch
¹/₂ cup rice milk
¹/₂ cup dairy-free, soy-free vegetable shortening

¹/₂ cup caster sugar (very fine)
¹/₂ teaspoon pure vanilla extract

1. Whisk together the cornstarch and rice milk in a small heavy saucepan until smooth, being sure to whisk out any lumps.

2. Bring to just below a simmer (a scald) over medium-low heat, stirring continuously with a wooden spoon, until it thickens (this happens very quickly, in about 1 minute or less). Remove from the heat and stir vigorously until smooth. Set aside to cool.

3. In the bowl of a stand mixer fitted with the paddle attachment, cream the shortening and caster sugar on medium speed for 3 minutes, then add the vanilla. Continue to beat while adding the cooled rice milk mixture, until fully incorporated, about 1 minute, stopping to scrape down the sides as necessary. Beat for 2 to 3 more minutes, or until light and fluffy, making sure you've whipped out any lumps. Serve at room temperature (it solidifies when chilled).

Banana Cake

MAKES 1 9-INCH CAKE

Tender, moist, and so easy to make, this cake is great as an after-school snack or at teatime, but it also makes a fabulous easy breakfast. It reminds me of Sara Lee Banana Cake, which my mom used to keep in the freezer for those times she wasn't baking. I was always sneaking a sliver.

3 cups Basic Gluten-Free Flour Mix (page 19)
3/4 teaspoon xanthan gum
1 1/2 teaspoons baking soda
1 1/2 teaspoons double-acting baking powder
1 teaspoon salt
1 teaspoon ground cinnamon
3/4 cup rice milk
2 teaspoons freshly squeezed lemon juice

4 ripe bananas, mashed (about 2 cups)
1/2 cup plus 2 1/2 tablespoons dairy-free, soy-free vegetable shortening
1 1/2 cups firmly packed light brown sugar
4 1/2 teaspoons Ener-G egg replacer mixed with 6 tablespoons rice milk
1 teaspoon pure vanilla extract

1. Preheat the oven to 350°F. Grease a 9 by 9-inch baking pan and dust lightly with flour mix, tapping out any extra.

2. Whisk together the flour mix, xanthan gum, baking soda, baking powder, salt, and cinnamon.

3. Combine the rice milk, lemon juice, and mashed banana, mixing well. Set aside.

4. In the bowl of a stand mixer fitted with the paddle attachment, cream the shortening on medium speed for about 2 minutes. Add the light brown sugar, mix, then add the egg replacer and vanilla. Beat well until completely combined, about 2 minutes.

5. Sift in the flour mixture in three batches, alternating with the rice milk/lemon juice/banana mixture, beginning and ending with the flour mixture. Mix until fully combined, about 30 seconds. Pour into the pan and smooth the surface.

6. Bake in the center of the oven for 45 minutes, or until the top is golden and a skewer inserted into the center of the cake comes out clean. Rotate the pan halfway through the baking time.

7. Let cool completely in the pan on a cooling rack. Once room temperature, cover with a large plate, invert the cake onto the plate, then reinvert onto the rack or serving plate. Store covered or wrapped at room temperature.

Christèle's Gâteau au Yaourt (French Yogurt Cake)

MAKES 1 9 BY 5-INCH CAKE

My French friend Christèle was kind enough to share her recipe for gâteau au yaourt. I have adapted it here to be allergen-free, but it doesn't suffer one bit. The beauty of this recipe is in its simplicity. It is easy, fast, and clean. You use the yogurt container (called "measure" in the recipe) as a measuring tool. Feel free to experiment with adding additional flavors to this cake, such as lemon or orange zest, or more rum, brandy, or cardamom. It's a great basic template to play with.

1 (6-ounce) container vanilla vegan yogurt

1½ "measures" granulated sugar

1 tablespoon Ener-G egg replacer mixed with ¼ cup rice milk

1 "measure" canola oil

3 "measures" Basic Gluten-Free Flour Mix (page 19) (unlike all the other recipes in this book, you should scoop the flour, instead of spooning it into the measuring cup)

½ teaspoon xanthan gum

1 teaspoon double-acting baking powder

¼ teaspoon salt

1 teaspoon pure vanilla extract

1 tablespoon rum (optional)

1. Preheat the oven to 350°F. Grease a 9 by 5-inch loaf pan and sprinkle with a little flour mix, tapping out any extra.

2. In the bowl of a stand mixer fitted with the paddle attachment, combine all the ingredients, adding them one at a time in the order listed above, beating on medium speed after each addition. Beat until smooth, about 1 minute. Pour into the loaf pan and bake in the center of the oven for about 1 hour and 10 minutes, or until the top is a lovely golden color and a toothpick inserted into the center comes out dry. Rotate the pan halfway through the baking time.

3. Let cool completely in the pan on a cooling rack before turning out. Slice with a sharp serrated knife.

Spongecake

MAKES 1 10-INCH CAKE

I learned from my mother that the easiest dessert to bake for a dinner party is a simple sponge-cake. It takes almost no time and can be dressed up to look quite fancy. This not-too-sweet cake can be served with fresh berries or compote and topped with a dollop of Vegan Whipped Topping (page 113) for a light finish to any meal.

1 tablespoon Ener-G egg replacer mixed with
  1/4 cup rice milk
11/2 cups granulated sugar
1 tablespoon pure vanilla extract
3 tablespoons canola oil

3 cups Basic Gluten-Free Flour Mix (page 19)
3/4 teaspoon xanthan gum
4 teaspoons double-acting baking powder
1/2 teaspoon salt
1 cup warm rice milk

1. Preheat the oven to 350°F. Grease a 10-inch Bundt pan or tube pan, and dust with a little flour mix, tapping out any extra.

2. In the bowl of a stand mixer fitted with the paddle attachment, whisk the egg replacer until foamy, about 1 minute. Add the sugar, vanilla, and canola oil, and beat on medium speed for 2 minutes.

3. In a separate bowl, whisk together the flour mix, xanthan gum, baking powder, and salt.

4. Add the dry ingredients to the wet, alternating with the rice milk, mixing on low until smooth, about 1 minute. Pour into the pan, and bake in the center of the oven for about 40 minutes, or until golden on top and a skewer inserted into the center of the cake comes out clean. Rotating the pan halfway through the baking time. Turn out immediately onto a cooling rack and let cool to room temperature before slicing.

Lemon Poppy Seed Bundt Cake with Lemon Glaze

MAKES 1 10-INCH CAKE

This fabulous low-fat teacake is a favorite with kids and grown-ups alike. My sons like it for break-fast with a glass of rice milk, I prefer it in the afternoon with a nice cup of tea, and my husband eats his with a scoop of Vanilla Rice Dream for dessert. Make it a day in advance so the flavors meld.

3/4 cup rice milk

1/4 cup freshly squeezed lemon juice

Zest of 1 lemon

2 cups granulated sugar

1 tablespoon Ener-G egg replacer mixed with
    1/4 cup rice milk

3 tablespoons canola oil

2 teaspoons yellow food coloring (see Resources,
    page 177)

3 cups Basic Gluten-Free Flour Mix (page 19)

3/4 teaspoon xanthan gum

4 teaspoons double-acting baking powder

1/2 teaspoon salt

1/4 cup poppy seeds

1 recipe Lemon Glaze (recipe follows)

1. Preheat the oven to 350°F. Grease a 10-inch Bundt pan, and dust with a little flour mix, tapping out any extra.

2. Combine the rice milk, lemon juice, and lemon zest and set aside.

3. In the bowl of a stand mixer fitted with the paddle attachment, cream the sugar and egg replacer on medium speed. Beat until fluffy, about 2 minutes. Add the canola oil and food coloring, and mix until lemon colored, about 1 minute.

4. In a separate bowl, combine the flour mix, xanthan gum, baking powder, and salt.

5. Add the dry ingredients to the wet, alternating with the rice milk mixture, mixing on low until smooth, about 1 minute. Fold in the poppy seeds.

6. Pour the batter into the Bundt pan. Bake in the center of the oven for 50 minutes, or until lightly golden on top and the edges are a light golden brown and pulling away slightly from the pan, rotating the pan halfway through. Remove from the oven, let cool in the pan for about 5 minutes, then invert onto a cooling rack to finish cooling. Let cool to room temperature before glazing. Let the glaze set before covering the cake. Store on the counter, not in the fridge, or it will dry out. Let rest overnight to meld the flavors.

Lemon Glaze ■ MAKES 1/3 CUP

1 cup confectioner's sugar

2 to 3 tablespoons freshly squeezed lemon juice

Combine the confectioners' sugar and lemon juice, adding 1 tablespoon of juice at a time, until the glaze is smooth and thin enough to drizzle.

Carrot Pineapple Bundt Cake with Sucanat Glaze

MAKES 1 10-INCH CAKE

This rich and highly nutritious cake is loaded with vitamin C and vitamin A. It's moist and keeps well for days.

2 cups Sucanat or brown sugar

4¹/₂ teaspoons Ener-G egg replacer mixed with 6 tablespoons rice milk

1¹/₂ cups canola oil

1 teaspoon pure vanilla extract

2 cups finely shredded carrots

1 cup crushed pineapple, undrained

3¹/₄ cups Basic Gluten-Free Flour Mix (page 19)

1 teaspoon xanthan gum

2 teaspoons double-acting baking powder

1 teaspoon baking soda

¹/₂ teaspoon salt

2 teaspoons ground cinnamon

1 teaspoon ground nutmeg

1 recipe Sucanat Glaze (recipe follows)

1. Preheat the oven to 350°F. Grease a 10-inch Bundt pan, and dust with a little flour mix, tapping out any extra.

2. In a large bowl, combine the Sucanat, egg replacer, canola oil, and vanilla. Mix well for about 1 minute. Stir in the carrots and pineapple.

3. In a separate bowl, whisk together the flour mix, xanthan gum, baking powder, baking soda, salt, cinnamon, and nutmeg.

4. Fold the dry ingredients into the wet and mix well for about 1 minute. Pour the batter into the pan and bake for 1 hour and 10 minutes, rotating the pan halfway through. Bake until a skewer inserted into the center of the cake comes out clean. Cool in the pan for 10 minutes. Loosen the edges with a frosting spatula or knife and turn out onto a cooling rack. Let cool to warm, poke about 12 small holes in the top of the cake using the skewer. Spoon the glaze over the top of the cake, being sure to spoon it into the holes. Let the cake cool completely to room temperature and for the glaze to set before slicing.

Sucanat Glaze ■ MAKES ¹/₄ CUP

¹/₄ cup orange juice

3 tablespoons Sucanat or brown sugar

2 teaspoons dairy-free, soy-free vegetable shortening

1 teaspoon orange zest

Combine the orange juice and Sucanat in a small saucepan. Bring to a simmer over medium heat. Once it comes to a simmer, cook, stirring, for about 3 minutes, or until it becomes syrupy. Remove from the heat and stir in the shortening and zest. Let cool for a few minutes before pouring over the warm cake.

Orange Chiffon Cake with Orange Rum Sauce

MAKES 1 10-INCH CAKE

This is a sophisticated cake that also gets "two thumbs up!" from my kids. I've been told it tastes like pound cake, but because it's made with canola oil, not butter, it's really a vegan chiffon cake. Chiffon cakes are very moist, and do not tend to harden or dry out as much as cakes made with butter or shortening, because the oil stays liquid, even at cooler temperatures. Chiffon cakes are traditionally served with flavorful sauces or other accompaniments, such as chocolate or fruit fillings.

2 cups plus 1 tablespoon granulated sugar
1 tablespoon Ener-G egg replacer mixed with
   1/4 cup rice milk
1 cup orange juice
2 tablespoons orange zest
3 tablespoons canola oil

3 cups Basic Gluten-Free Flour Mix (page 19)
3/4 teaspoon xanthan gum
4 teaspoons double-acting baking powder
1/2 teaspoon salt
1 recipe Orange Rum Sauce (recipe follows)

1. Preheat the oven to 350°F. Grease a 10-inch tube pan or Bundt pan, and dust with a little flour mix, tapping out any extra.

2. In the bowl of a stand mixer fitted with the paddle attachment, combine 2 cups of the sugar and the egg replacer. Beat on medium speed for about 1 minute.

3. Add the orange juice, orange zest, and canola oil. Mix for about 1 minute more.

4. In a separate bowl, combine the flour mix, xanthan gum, baking powder, and salt.

5. Sift the dry ingredients into the wet in three batches, mixing after each addition. Mix until smooth, about 1 minute.

6. Pour the batter into the pan. Sprinkle the remaining 1 tablespoon sugar evenly over the top.

7. Bake in the center of the oven for 40 minutes, or until lovely golden brown on top, rotating the pan halfway through. Let cool in the pan for 5 minutes before inverting onto a cooling rack. Let cool to room temperature. Place the cake on a cake stand or serving plate. Poke about 24 holes into the cake, and spoon about half of the sauce over the top and sides, being sure to drizzle it into the holes so it sinks in. Reserve the remaining sauce to serve along with slices of cake. This cake is best the day it's made. Store covered in the fridge.

CONTINUED

Orange Rum Sauce ■ MAKES 1¹/₃ CUPS

1/2 cup sugar
2 tablespoons cornstarch
Pinch of salt
1 cup orange juice

1/4 cup amber rum
1 tablespoon dairy-free, soy-free vegetable
  shortening
1 teaspoon pure vanilla extract

Whisk together the sugar, cornstarch, and salt in a small saucepan. Whisk in the orange juice and rum, and bring to a simmer over medium heat, stirring continuously, until it thickens slightly, about 5 minutes. Remove from the heat and stir in the shortening and vanilla.

6

PIES, TARTS, CRISPS, CRUMBLES, *Cobblers, Puddings, Betties,* AND BUCKLES

My mother taught me that the easiest way to justify dessert is to include fruit in it. This allows you to say, "Have another helping, it's *good* for you!" And it's true; it is good for you to eat a wide variety of colorful, phytonutrient-rich, fiber-packed fruits and berries. I love to bake what's in season, so you'll find recipes here for seasonal produce all year round: apples, cranberries, pumpkin, and pears for fall and winter, a multitude of berries in spring, and plums and peaches in the summer. These fruits are all at their peak and least expensive when in season, but these desserts can also be made any time of year with frozen fruit, so bake whatever you want, whenever you want, to your heart's content.

Not only is this chapter full of über-healthful desserts, but it's also filled with recipes that really show off the merits of gluten-free baking, which especially shines with pies and tarts. Gluten-free flour makes beautiful, dependable, delicious crusts. In fact, I'd venture to say, they're better than their wheat flour counterparts. They are quick to make because the dough doesn't need chilling, they don't need pie weights

CONTINUED

or beans for prebaking, and they remain tender and flaky for days. Feel free to use these crust recipes for any pie or tart of your choice. The Cornmeal Pâte Brisée (page 141) is particularly easy to work with, and pairs well with sweet or savory filling. I also encourage you to mix and match the crisp, crumble, and cobbler toppings. If you want to include more protein, use the topping from the Maple Apple Crumble (page 148), which is made with quinoa flakes, a complete protein grain. For a traditional old-school crisp topping, use the topping from the Peach Blueberry Crisp (page 147). And if you want to avoid any refined sugar, use the topping from the Mixed Berry Crisp (page 145). For a lower-fat option, use the Cobbler Biscuit Dough (page 149). I've said it before, I'll say it again—there's something here for everyone.

Blueberry Pie

MAKES 1 9-INCH PIE

I know they say apple pie is about as American as you can get, but I give that moniker to blueberry pie instead. When I think of pie, I think summertime and blueberries! Every summer, we visit my father in western Massachusetts and go to a big field with the most prolific old blueberry bushes you've ever seen, and fill our buckets with heaping cups of blueberries. We eat a lot of them right then and there while picking, but the rest get made into pancakes, and best of all, baked up into pie!

Blueberry Pie Filling

6 cups fresh or frozen blueberries

3/4 cup granulated sugar

1/4 cup Basic Gluten-Free Flour Mix (page 19)

1/8 teaspoon salt

2 tablespoons freshly squeezed lime juice

2 tablespoons dairy-free, soy-free vegetable shortening

Double Flaky Pie Crust

3 cups Basic Gluten-Free Flour Mix (page 19)

6 tablespoons sweet rice flour

3 tablespoons confectioners' sugar

1 1/2 teaspoons xanthan gum

3/4 teaspoon salt

1 1/4 cups dairy-free, soy-free vegetable shortening

4 1/2 teaspoons Ener-G egg replacer mixed with 6 tablespoons rice milk

2 tablespoons freshly squeezed lemon juice

1 tablespoon rice milk, for brushing top crust

1 tablespoon granulated sugar, for sprinkling over top of pie

1. Set the oven rack in the lowest position, place a baking sheet on the rack, and preheat the oven to 425°F.

2. To make the filling, combine the blueberries, granulated sugar, flour mix, salt, and lime juice. Toss gently. Set aside.

3. To make the pie crust, in the bowl of a stand mixer fitted with the paddle attachment, whisk together the flours, confectioners' sugar, xanthan gum, and salt. Add the shortening in tablespoon-size pieces, and mix on medium speed until you have a coarse meal, about 1 minute. Add the egg replacer and lemon juice and mix until combined (it should start to ball in the center of the bowl), about 1 minute.

4. Divide the dough in half and mold into two balls. Set one aside. Place the other on a sheet of parchment paper. Flatten into a disk, pinching together the edges. Top with a second piece of parchment paper, and roll out to 1/4 inch thick and about 2 inches wider than your pie dish. Grease a 9-inch pie dish lightly with a little vegetable shortening. Remove the top sheet of parchment paper, flip the crust into the pie dish, pressing down

CONTINUED

with the palm of your hand and using your fingers to press into the dish around the edges, then peel off the other sheet of parchment paper. Trim the edges, patching as necessary. Prick the bottom 8 times with a fork and refrigerate while you roll out the second crust.

5. Roll out the second crust the same way you did the first.

6. Pour the filling into the bottom crust. Cut the shortening into little pieces and dot on top of the berries. Remove the top sheet of parchment paper from the rolled-out top crust, and flip on top of the pie. Press down along the edges with your fingers to secure the top crust. Peel off the remaining sheet of parchment paper. Seal and crimp the edges. Use the tines of a fork to make a final seal all the way around. Using a sharp knife, cut 6 slits in the top of the pie. At this point, I often gather up the scraps of dough, roll them to 1/4 inch thick between two sheets of parchment paper, cut them into 1-inch decorative shapes such as leaves or stars with a small cookie cutter, and adorn the top of the crust. Brush the crust, including the outer edge, with the rice milk. Sprinkle evenly with the granulated sugar.

7. Place the pie on the preheated baking sheet. Bake at 425°F for about 25 minutes, or until the crust is golden. Reduce the temperature to 400°F if the crust is browning too quickly.

8. Rotate the baking sheet, decrease the temperature to 375°F, and bake for about 45 minutes longer, or until the fruit is really bubbling up through the slits on top and the crust is deeply golden. If you have used frozen blueberries, it will take a little longer. If the edges of your crust are browning too quickly, cover with a little loose aluminum foil, or better yet, a pie shield.

9. Remove from the oven and let cool on a cooling rack to room temperature, at least 2 hours, before cutting into wedges.

Tip ■ If you are an enthusiastic pie maker, I encourage you to invest in a good pie dish. I've been using the same 9-inch Emile Henry Auberge pie dish I got as a wedding gift for years, with endless success. They are sturdy and versatile, and make for a great presentation.

Cranberry Apple Pie

MAKES 1 9-INCH PIE

As a Cape Codder, I'm crazy about cranberries. And "apple" was my son Lennon's first word, so you know how we feel about them in our house! This pie is the perfect combination of tart and sweet. It is an ideal dessert to end any holiday meal. It is extremely pretty, with its tiers of fruit and deep golden crust. Look for firm, sweet apples to balance the tartness of the cranberries. I like Braeburn, Fuji, or Jonagold. To make this dessert completely refined sugar–free, double the proportions for the Single Flaky Sucanat Pie Crust recipe (page 130) and roll out as instructed below.

Cranberry Layer
2 cups cranberries
1/4 cup orange juice
1/3 cup light agave nectar
1/4 teaspoon ground cinnamon
1/4 teaspoon salt
3 tablespoons water

Apple Layer
8 apples
2 tablespoons Basic Gluten-Free Flour Mix
  (page 19)
1/2 cup light agave nectar
1/4 teaspoon ground cinnamon
1/4 teaspoon salt

1 recipe Double Flaky Pie Crust (page 125)
1 tablespoon rice milk, for brushing top crust
1 tablespoon sugar, for sprinkling over top
  crust

1. To make the cranberry layer, combine the cranberries, orange juice, agave nectar, cinnamon, and salt in a medium saucepan over medium-high heat. Cook, stirring, for 8 to 10 minutes, breaking up the berries against the side of the pan and smoothing as much as possible. Remove from the heat and stir in the water. Let cool for 30 minutes.

2. To make the apple layer, peel, core, and cut the apples into 1/4-inch-thick slices. In a large microwave-safe bowl, gently toss the apple slices with the flour mix, agave nectar, cinnamon, and salt. Microwave on high for 9 minutes, tossing gently every 3 minutes, until the juices are thickened and glossy. Remove from the microwave and let cool to room temperature, about 30 minutes.

3. Meanwhile, set the oven rack in the lowest position, place a baking sheet on the rack, and preheat the oven to 425°F.

4. Make the Double Flaky Pie Crust as instructed on page 125, up through rolling out the bottom crust. Grease a 9-inch pie dish with a little vegetable shortening. Remove the top sheet of parchment paper, flip the crust into the pie dish, pressing down with the palm of your hand and using your fingers to press into the dish around the edges, then peel

CONTINUED

off the other sheet of parchment paper. Trim the edges, patching as necessary. Prick the bottom 8 times with a fork.

5. Spread the cranberry mixture evenly across the bottom crust. Spread the apple mixture over the cranberry mixture, mounding it slightly in the center.

6. Roll out the second crust the same way you did the first. Remove the top sheet of parchment paper from the rolled-out top crust, and flip on top of the pie. Press down along the edges with your fingers to secure the top crust. Peel off the remaining sheet of parchment paper. Seal and crimp the edges. Then either trim and flute the edges with your thumb and forefinger or use the tines of a fork to make a final seal all the way around. Cut four $1\frac{1}{2}$-inch slits in the top crust, north, south, east, and west, cutting outward from the center. At this point, I often gather up the scraps of dough, roll them to $\frac{1}{4}$ inch thick between two sheets of parchment paper, cut them into 1-inch decorative shapes such as leaves or stars with a small cookie cutter, and adorn the top of the crust. Brush the crust, including the outer edge, with the rice milk. Sprinkle evenly with the sugar.

7. Place the pie on the preheated baking sheet and bake for 25 minutes at 425°F, or until the crust is turning golden; reduce the temperature to 400°F if the crust is browning too quickly. Rotate the baking sheet, decrease the temperature to 375°F, and bake for about 25 minutes longer, or until the top is a rich golden color and the fruit is beginning to bubble up through the slits. If the edges of the crust are browning too quickly, cover loosely with foil, or better yet, cover with a pie shield.

8. Remove the pie from the oven and let cool on a cooling rack for at least 2 hours before cutting into wedges. I like this pie best at room temperature.

Pumpkin Pie

MAKES 1 9-INCH PIE

This is not your mama's pumpkin pie! This vegan spin on the old-fashioned favorite is light, fresh, and decidedly modern. I consider this one of my greatest achievements in this book, because I was able to make pumpkin pie without eggs, and without tofu, which is the usual substitute in vegan baking. I much prefer this version of pumpkin pie to the one I grew up on, because it's not too rich and is made without refined sugar, making it a treat my whole family can indulge in, until we've eaten every last crumb!

Single Flaky Sucanat Pie Crust

1 1/2 cups Basic Gluten-Free Flour Mix (page 19)

3 tablespoons sweet rice flour

1 1/2 tablespoons Sucanat or brown sugar

3/4 teaspoon xanthan gum

1/4 teaspoon plus 1/8 teaspoon salt

1/2 cup plus 2 tablespoons dairy-free, soy-free vegetable shortening

2 1/4 teaspoons Ener-G egg replacer mixed with 3 tablespoons rice milk

1 tablespoon freshly squeezed lemon juice

Pumpkin Pie Filling

2 cups pumpkin purée

2 tablespoons canola oil

3/4 cup Sucanat or brown sugar

1/3 cup maple syrup

1/2 teaspoon salt

1 teaspoon pure vanilla extract

2 teaspoons grated fresh ginger

1/2 teaspoon ground cinnamon

1/4 teaspoon ground nutmeg

2 1/2 cups chilled rice milk

1/4 cup cornstarch

1 (0.3-ounce) packet vegan gelatin

1. Preheat the oven to 375°F.

2. To make the pie crust, in the bowl of a stand mixer fitted with the paddle attachment, whisk together the flours, Sucanat, xanthan gum, and salt.

3. Add the shortening and mix on medium speed until you have a coarse meal, about 1 minute. Add the egg replacer and lemon juice and mix until combined (it should start to ball in the center of the bowl), about 1 minute.

4. Turn out the dough onto a sheet of parchment paper, mold into a ball, flatten into a disk, pinching together the edges, and top with another sheet of parchment paper. Roll out to 1/4 inch thick and about 2 inches wider than your pie dish. Grease a 9-inch pie dish with a little vegetable shortening. Remove the top sheet of parchment paper, flip the crust into the pie dish, pressing down with the palm of your hand and using your fingers to press into the dish around the edges, then peel off the other sheet of parchment paper. Trim and flute the edges, patching as necessary. Prick the bottom 8 times with a fork.

5. Bake the crust in the center of the oven for 25 minutes, or until lightly golden. Transfer to a cooling rack, and let cool to room temperature.

6. To make the filling, combine the pumpkin, canola oil, Sucanat, maple syrup, salt, vanilla, ginger, cinnamon, nutmeg, and 1/4 cup of the rice milk in a heavy saucepan, whisking together well. Bring to a simmer over medium heat, then decrease the heat to medium-low, and cook, stirring, for 5 minutes.

7. Whisk together the cornstarch and 1/4 cup more of the rice milk. Pour into the pumpkin mixture and cook, stirring, for about 2 more minutes. Whisk vigorously to smooth out any lumps. Remove from the heat and set aside.

8. Whisk the vegan gelatin into the remaining 2 cups rice milk. Pour into a small saucepan. Bring to a full boil over medium-high heat, stirring often.

9. Working quickly, pour the gelatin mixture into the pumpkin mixture, stirring well to combine thoroughly, then pour into the room-temperature pie shell.

10. Transfer to the fridge. Chill for at least 2 hours before serving. Cut into wedges. Eat plain or with a little Vegan Whipped Topping (page 113).

Tip ■ Crusts are like people—they have moods! Sometimes they're even-tempered and roll out smoothly and easily. Other days, they fall apart. It depends on the temperature, the humidity level, the brands of flour and shortening, and perhaps, the randomness of life. Do not dismay if your crust is perfect one day, but the next time you make the very same recipe it breaks apart a bit. Just patch it back together and nobody will ever know.

Banana Cream Pie

MAKES 1 9-INCH PIE

Banana cream pie was always one of my favorite desserts as a child, and now it's a favorite of my son Lennon, too. The yellow food coloring is optional, but it mimics the lovely creamy hue imparted by traditional egg yolks in custard. Coconut milk makes a great vegan custard, and pairs beautifully with the bananas. If you prefer, you may use rice milk instead for a much lighter pie.

Single Flaky Pie Crust

1½ cups Basic Gluten-Free Flour Mix
   (page 19)

3 tablespoons sweet rice flour

1½ tablespoons confectioners' sugar

¾ teaspoon xanthan gum

¼ teaspoon plus ⅛ teaspoon salt

½ cup plus 2 tablespoons dairy-free, soy-free
   vegetable shortening

2¼ teaspoons Ener-G egg replacer mixed with
   3 tablespoons rice milk

1 tablespoon freshly squeezed lemon juice

Banana Cream Pie Filling

19 ounces coconut milk (either use 1 [19-ounce]
   can or measure out 19 ounces from
   2 smaller cans, but be sure to stir each can
   up first to mix in the coconut cream)

¼ cup dark Karo syrup

¼ cup cornstarch

½ cup granulated sugar

¼ teaspoon salt

1 teaspoon yellow food coloring (optional, try
   Seelect Natural Yellow Food Coloring, made
   with turmeric; see Resources, page 177)

1 teaspoon pure vanilla extract

1 tablespoon Ener-G egg replacer mixed with
   ¼ cup rice milk

3 to 4 ripe bananas, thinly sliced

1. Preheat the oven to 375°F.

2. To make the pie crust, in the bowl of a stand mixer fitted with the paddle attachment, whisk together the flours, sugar, xanthan gum, and salt.

3. Add the shortening and mix on medium speed until you have a coarse meal, about 1 minute.

4. Add the egg replacer and lemon juice and mix until combined (it should start to ball in the center of the bowl), about 1 minute.

5. Turn out the dough onto a sheet of parchment paper, mold into a ball, flatten into a disk, pinching together the edges, and top with another sheet of parchment paper. Roll out to ¼ inch thick and about 2 inches wider than your pie dish. Grease a 9-inch pie dish with a little vegetable shortening. Remove the top sheet of parchment paper, flip the crust into the pie dish, pressing down with the palm of your hand and using your fingers to press into the dish around the edges, then peel off the other sheet of parchment paper. Trim and flute the edges, patching as necessary. Prick the bottom 8 times with a fork.

6. Bake the crust in the center of the oven for 25 minutes, or until lightly golden. Remove and let cool completely on a cooling rack before filling.

7. To make the filling, set aside 1/4 cup of the coconut milk. Combine the remaining coconut milk and Karo syrup in a heavy saucepan over medium heat. Heat, stirring, until it begins to bubble around the edges. Remove from the heat.

8. In a separate bowl, whisk together the reserved 1/4 cup coconut milk, cornstarch, sugar, salt, yellow food coloring, and vanilla.

9. Add the egg replacer to the coconut milk/Karo mixture, stir, then add the cornstarch mixture. Heat over medium heat, stirring continuously, until it comes to a simmer. Cook, stirring continuously, for about 4 minutes, or until thickened.

10. Spread a small amount of the custard in the bottom of the pie shell. Place a layer of sliced banana on top of the custard. Spread half of the remaining custard over the bananas, add another layer of bananas, and then top with the remaining custard. Smooth the top and let cool to room temperature. Refrigerate, covered, until ready to serve.

Tip ■ For a lighter, lower-fat pie, use 2 cups rice milk in place of the coconut milk and add 1 tablespoon shortening to the saucepan with the rice milk and Karo syrup.

Chocolate Pudding Tart

MAKES 1 9½-INCH TART

My friend Amy has celiac disease and a dairy allergy. She says this tart is just perfect, and makes her feel "normal" again. She loves that she can share it with her non-food-allergic husband and kids, and that they gobble it just as voraciously. The shortbread crust is heavenly with the rich chocolate pudding.

1 Shortbread Tart Crust, prebaked and cooled (recipe follows)

¾ cup granulated sugar

⅓ cup cornstarch

½ teaspoon salt

2½ cups rice milk

1 tablespoon Ener-G egg replacer

2 ounces unsweetened baking chocolate, cut into small pieces (a serrated knife works best to break it up)

½ teaspoon pure vanilla extract

1. Prepare the Shortbread Tart Crust.

2. Whisk together the sugar, cornstarch, and salt in a heavy saucepan. Add the rice milk, whisking until fully combined. Add the egg replacer, whisking until light and frothy.

3. Set the saucepan over medium heat. Warm slightly, add the chocolate pieces, and cook, whisking, until it comes to a slow simmer and has thickened, about 5 minutes. If it lumps at all, just whisk more vigorously.

4. Once it has thickened to a pudding consistency, reduce the heat to medium-low and cook, just below a simmer (a scald), stirring with a wooden spoon, for 20 minutes, until it has thickened almost to a soft ball stage. The pudding should be dark and chocolaty, and should slowly drip off of a wooden spoon. The pudding must reach this thick rich stage or it will not set, so it's better to err on the side of cooking a little longer than not long enough. Once really thick, remove from the heat, whisk in the vanilla, and pour into the tart crust.

5. Chill thoroughly in the refrigerator, 3 to 4 hours. Serve as is or with Vegan Whipped Topping (page 113). Store, covered, in the refrigerator.

CONTINUED

Shortbread Tart Crust ■ MAKES 1 9 1/2-INCH TART CRUST

1 1/2 cups Basic Gluten-Free Flour Mix
  (page 19)
1/4 cup plus 2 tablespoons confectioners'
  sugar
3/4 teaspoon xanthan gum

1/8 teaspoon salt
10 tablespoons dairy-free, soy free vegetable
  shortening
2 tablespoons orange juice

1. In the bowl of a stand mixer fitted with the paddle attachment, whisk together the flour mix, confectioners' sugar, xanthan gum, and salt.

2. Add the shortening in tablespoon-sized pieces (be very exact about this measurement, being sure not to add any more than instructed), and mix on medium speed until you have a coarse meal, about 1 minute.

3. Add the orange juice and mix until the dough begins to ball in the center, about 20 seconds.

4. Turn out onto a sheet of parchment paper, form into a ball, top with another sheet of parchment paper, flatten into a disk, and roll out into a circle about 1/4 inch thick and 1 inch wider than your tart pan.

5. Lightly grease a 9 1/2-inch nonstick tart pan with a removable bottom. Remove the top sheet of parchment paper, flip the crust into the pan, and press down with the palm of your hand. Gently peel off the remaining sheet of parchment paper, and finish pressing the dough into the pan, patching the sides as necessary. If the dough crumbles a bit or breaks apart, don't worry about it, just patch it back together—it will still bake up to be a lovely crust! Trim by running a rolling pin over the top of the tart pan. Prick the crust 8 times with a fork.

6. To prebake the crust, preheat the oven to 350°F and bake for 20 minutes, until set and very lightly golden. Let cool completely on a cooling rack before filling.

Mixed Berry Tart

MAKES 1 9½-INCH TART

There is nothing more delicious than custard cream and fresh berries, as far as I'm concerned. I could eat it with a spoon, morning, noon, and night. This light, fresh tart is easy to make and a favorite with all ages. My kids adore the shortbread crust, because it tastes like cookies and it's heaped with antioxidant-rich berries, making it rather virtuous (well, sort of . . .).

1 Shortbread Tart Crust, prebaked and cooled (page 136)

¼ cup seedless jelly or jam (I like red currant jelly or seedless blackberry or raspberry preserves)

Pastry Custard

1 cup coconut milk (or rice milk, for a lighter custard)

2 tablespoons dark Karo syrup

2 tablespoons cornstarch

¼ cup granulated sugar

⅛ teaspoon salt

½ teaspoon pure vanilla extract

1½ teaspoons Ener-G egg replacer mixed with 2 tablespoons rice milk

3 cups assorted berries (at least three types; if using strawberries, halve them)

1. Prepare the Shortbread Tart Crust.

2. Warm the jelly in the microwave or a small saucepan, whisking it to thin it out.

3. Using a pastry brush, spread the jelly over the bottom of the crust. Chill in the refrigerator for 10 minutes to set.

4. To make the pastry custard, combine 3/4 cup of the coconut milk and Karo syrup in a heavy saucepan. Warm over medium-high heat, whisking until it starts to simmer around the edges. Remove from the heat.

5. Whisk together the remaining ¼ cup coconut milk and the cornstarch in a small bowl, stirring until smooth. Add the sugar, salt, and vanilla.

6. Add the egg replacer and cornstarch mixture to the pan with the coconut milk/Karo mixture and bring to a simmer over medium heat, whisking continuously. Once the mixture comes to a simmer, cook for 1 minute, stirring; it will thicken quickly. Remove from the heat and let cool for a few minutes.

7. Remove the crust from the fridge. Fill the shell with the custard mixture. Arrange the berries in pretty concentric circles, or scatter in a more free-form fashion, being sure to top the custard completely with fruit.

Tip ■ Coconut milk has a tendency to separate. Before using, open the can, empty the contents into a bowl, and whisk thoroughly to reintegrate the cream. Then measure out.

Brandied Peach Tart

MAKES 1 9¹/₂-INCH TART

This lovely tart is great made during peach season, when peaches are at their peak. It can also be made with frozen peaches, but most store-bought brands are underripe and bland. If using frozen peaches, be sure to macerate them a little longer in the syrup/brandy mixture to soften them up. Test for readiness after the first 30 minutes, and continue to macerate as long as necessary, but not so long that they become mushy.

1 Shortbread Tart Crust, prebaked and cooled (page 136)

4 or 5 peaches, ripe but still firm

3/4 cup water

3/4 cup granulated sugar

7¹/2 tablespoons brandy

3/4 cup peach jam

1. Prepare the Shortbread Tart Crust.

2. Blanch the peaches by bringing a pot of water to a boil (make sure the pot is large enough to fit 2 peaches at a time). Place 2 peaches in the boiling water. Let boil for 40 seconds. Remove the peaches with a slotted spoon and plunge into a bowl of ice water, then remove to drain. Repeat with the remaining peaches. Peel using a sharp paring knife or just use your fingers. The peach skin should slip off easily. Cut the peaches in half, remove the pit, and slice into 8- to 10 ¹/2-inch-thick slices. Pat the slices dry.

    To use frozen peaches, select 40 to 45 pretty slices, and defrost in a single layer on paper towels for at least 1 hour, or until completely defrosted. Pat dry. Whole Foods 365 Organic Frozen Peaches has scored highest in the taste tests I've seen, but I'm still searching for a better frozen peach.

3. Combine the water and sugar in a small saucepan over medium heat and bring to a simmer to make a simple syrup. Once dissolved, remove from the heat and stir in 6 tablespoons of the brandy.

4. Put the peach slices in a shallow bowl and pour the syrup over them, tossing gently and making sure all slices are covered. Let macerate for 30 minutes to soak up the brandy flavor.

5. Drain the peaches and gently pat dry with paper towels. Using the largest slices first, make a circle with the peaches in the bottom of the crust, starting at the outer edge of the crust and slightly overlapping the slices. Working inward, make about 3 circles total, using the smallest slices last to make a final spiral of fruit.

6. Heat the peach jam in a small saucepan over medium heat, stirring continuously, or warm in the microwave in a microwave-safe bowl, stopping to stir the jam at 30-second increments. You want to break up any large lumps of fruit and thin out the jam so it's easy to spread. Add the remaining $1^1/_2$ tablespoons brandy and combine thoroughly.

7. Using a pastry brush, spread the jam over the fruit to create a glossy finish.

8. Chill the tart in the fridge to set. Once set, store in the fridge loosely covered with foil or plastic wrap. This is delicious with Vanilla Rice Dream or Vegan Whipped Topping (page 113).

Pear Blackberry Tart

MAKES 1 9¹/₂-INCH TART

This is a simple, elegant, not-too-sweet dessert that you can whip up in no time. I recommend using Bosc or Anjou pears in this recipe, because they hold their shape when baked.

1 recipe Single Flaky Pie Crust (page 132)
1¹/₂ pounds Bosc or Anjou pears, ripe but still
    firm (about 3 large)
¹/₂ cup plus 2 tablespoons granulated sugar

1 tablespoon freshly squeezed lemon juice
2 tablespoons cornstarch
¹/₂ pint blackberries (5.6 to 6 ounces)

1. Preheat the oven to 375°F. Lightly grease a 9¹/₂-inch nonstick tart pan with a removable bottom.

2. Prepare the pie crust as instructed on page 132 up through step 4. Turn out the dough onto a sheet of parchment paper, mold into a ball, flatten into a disk, pinching together the edges, and top with another sheet of parchment paper. Roll out to ¹/₄ inch thick and about 1 inch wider than your tart pan.

3. Remove the top sheet of parchment paper, flip the crust into the pan, and press down with the palm of your hand. Gently peel off the remaining sheet of parchment paper and finish pressing the dough into the pan, patching the sides as necessary. If the dough crumbles a bit or breaks apart, just patch it back together—it will still bake up beautifully. Trim by running a rolling pin over the top of the tart pan. Prick the crust 8 times with a fork.

4. Partly prebake the crust in the center of the oven for 15 minutes, or until lightly golden. Transfer to a cooling rack and let come to room temperature.

5. While the tart crust cools, slice the pears in half lengthwise, then into quarters lengthwise. Cut out the core. Slice the quarters in half crosswise and then into 1¹/₂-inch by ¹/₂-inch slices.

6. Combine ¹/₂ cup of the sugar, the lemon juice, and the cornstarch in a large bowl, add the pear slices, and toss gently.

7. Fill the cooled tart crust with the pear mixture. Disperse the blackberries evenly among the pears. Sprinkle the top with the remaining 2 tablespoons sugar.

8. Bake in the center of the oven for about 1 hour, or until the pears have begun to caramelize a bit. Transfer to a cooling rack and let come to room temperature before cutting into wedges.

Raspberry Galette with Cornmeal Crust

MAKES 8 SERVINGS

This rustic free-from tart is great with raspberries, but you can just as easily substitute blueberries or blackberries. The cornmeal gives the crust a slightly crunchy texture, which complements the berries beautifully.

Cornmeal Pâte Brisée

1/3 cup rice milk

1 teaspoon freshly squeezed lemon juice

1 3/4 cups Basic Gluten-Free Flour Mix (page 19)

1/4 cup fine cornmeal

3/4 teaspoon xanthan gum

1/4 teaspoon salt

1/3 cup granulated sugar

1/2 cup dairy-free, soy-free vegetable shortening, chilled and cut into a 1/2-inch dice

1 tablespoon ice water, as necessary

Raspberry Filling

4 cups fresh or frozen raspberries

5 tablespoons granulated sugar

2 teaspoons freshly squeezed lemon juice

1/2 teaspoon ground cinnamon

2 tablespoons Basic Gluten-Free Flour Mix (page 19)

1 tablespoon rice milk, for brushing crust

1. To make the pâte brisée, combine the rice milk and lemon juice and set aside for 30 minutes.

2. Preheat the oven to 375°F.

3. Meanwhile, in the bowl of a stand mixer fitted with the paddle attachment, whisk together the flour mix, cornmeal, xanthan gum, and salt. Add the sugar, mixing for a few seconds until combined. Add the shortening, mixing on medium speed until you have a coarse meal, about 1 minute.

4. Slowly add the soured rice milk and mix on low speed until the dough begins to ball in the center, about 1 minute. If it seems too dry and is not coming together, add the ice water.

5. Turn the dough out onto a sheet of parchment paper. Mold into a ball, then flatten into a disk, pinching together the edges. Top with another sheet of parchment paper. Roll out the dough into a 13-inch circle. Place the dough and parchment on a baking sheet. Use your fingers to even out the edges if they're jagged. Remove the top piece of parchment paper.

6. To make the filling, combine the berries, 4 tablespoons of the sugar, lemon juice, cinnamon, and flour mix. Toss gently.

CONTINUED

7. Arrange the berries in the center of the dough, leaving a 2-inch border. Fold the edges of the dough toward the center (you can just lift the parchment from the outer edge to fold the dough), pressing gently to seal (the dough will only partially cover the fruit). Seal any cracks by pinching the crust with your fingers.

8. Using a pastry brush, brush the rice milk over the dough. Sprinkle the dough and the tops of the berries evenly with the remaining 1 tablespoon sugar.

9. Bake for 30 minutes in the center of the oven. Rotate the baking sheet, decrease the temperature to 350°F, and bake for 25 minutes longer, or until the pastry is golden. Transfer on the baking sheet to a cooling rack. Let come to room temperature before cutting into wedges.

Plum Cardamom Galette

MAKES 8 SERVINGS

A great way to bake with plums, this gorgeous free-form tart is a perfect light finish to any meal.

1 recipe Cornmeal Pâte Brisée (page 141)
2 pounds ripe but still firm red or black plums,
    halved, pitted, halves cut into 8 slices each
1/4 cup firmly packed light brown sugar
2 teaspoons freshly squeezed lemon juice

1/4 teaspoon ground cardamom
2 tablespoons cornstarch
Pinch of salt
1 tablespoon rice milk, for brushing crust
1 tablespoon granulated sugar, for sprinkling

1. Prepare the Cornmeal Pâte Brisée.

2. Preheat the oven to 375°F.

3. Combine the plums, light brown sugar, lemon juice, cardamom, cornstarch, and salt. Toss gently to coat evenly.

4. Transfer the rolled-out crust on parchment paper to a baking sheet. Remove the top sheet of parchment paper.

5. Arrange the plums in the center of the dough, leaving a 2-inch border. Fold the edges of dough toward the center (you can just lift the parchment from the outer edge to fold the dough), pressing gently to seal (the dough will only partially cover the fruit). Seal any cracks by pinching the crust with your fingers.

6. Using a pastry brush, brush the rice milk over the dough. Sprinkle the dough and the tops of the plums evenly with the granulated sugar.

7. Bake for 30 minutes in the center of the oven. Rotate the baking sheet, decrease the temperature to 350°F, and bake for 25 minutes longer, or until the pastry is golden. Transfer on the baking sheet to a cooling rack. Let come to room temperature before cutting into wedges.

Mixed Berry Crisp

MAKES 8 SERVINGS

This healthy crisp lasts well for several days (covered) on the counter. I'll often make one, serve it for dessert, and then dig in again the following morning for a gorgeous berry breakfast. It's made with natural unrefined sweeteners that are low on the glycemic index, and the berries and oats make for a nutritious, antioxidant-rich, fiber-packed treat. Fresh berries work best for this; if using frozen berries, defrost them for about 45 minutes and drain off any liquid that collects.

6 cups mixed berries

2 tablespoons freshly squeezed lemon juice

1/2 cup light agave nectar

2 tablespoons cornstarch

1/2 cup plus 2 tablespoons sweet rice flour

1/2 cup plus 2 tablespoons Basic Gluten-Free Flour Mix (page 19)

1/4 teaspoon xanthan gum

1 teaspoon double-acting baking powder

Pinch of salt

3/4 cup palm sugar, maple sugar, Sucanat, or firmly packed brown sugar

1 cup gluten-free old-fashioned oats or quinoa flakes

1/2 cup dairy-free, soy-free vegetable shortening

1. Preheat the oven to 350°F.

2. Gently toss the berries with the lemon juice and agave nectar. Sprinkle with the cornstarch and toss to coat evenly.

3. Grease an 11 by 7-inch or 8 by 8-inch baking dish. Transfer the berries to the baking dish, using a rubber spatula to scrape out all the agave/lemon juice.

4. Whisk together the flours, xanthan gum, baking powder, salt, and palm sugar. Add the oats and combine. Melt the shortening (30 to 60 seconds in the microwave does it). Add it to the dry ingredients, a little at a time, tossing between each addition. Mix until you have a large crumb. Sprinkle evenly over the berries.

5. Bake in the center of the oven for 30 minutes. Decrease the temperature to 325°F and bake for 20 minutes longer, or until the top is golden brown and the fruit is bubbling up around the sides. Let cool to room temperature before serving.

Peach Blueberry Crisp

MAKES 8 SERVINGS

Peaches and blueberries make a perfect pairing. Not only are they in season together, but their colors and flavors are also the ideal complement.

4 cups diced peaches, skin on
2 cups blueberries
2 tablespoons freshly squeezed lemon juice
1/2 cup light agave nectar
3/4 teaspoon ground cinnamon
2 tablespoons cornstarch
1 1/4 cups Basic Gluten-Free Flour Mix (page 19)

1/4 teaspoon xanthan gum
1/8 teaspoon salt
3/4 cup firmly packed brown sugar
1 cup gluten-free old-fashioned oats or quinoa flakes
1/2 cup dairy-free, soy-free vegetable shortening

1. Preheat the oven to 375°F.

2. Grease an 8 by 8-inch or 11 by 7-inch baking dish.

3. Combine the peaches and berries with the lemon juice and agave nectar, toss gently, then sprinkle in 1/2 teaspoon of the cinnamon and the cornstarch, stirring gently to combine. Transfer to the baking dish.

4. Combine the flour mix, xanthan gum, salt, and brown sugar. Whisk together, then add the remaining 1/4 teaspoon cinnamon and the oats. Toss well.

5. Melt the shortening (30 to 60 seconds in the microwave does it) and add it to the dry ingredients, a little at a time, tossing between each addition. Mix until you have a large crumb. Spread the crumb topping evenly over the fruit.

6. Bake in the center of the oven for about 40 minutes, or until the fruit is bubbling up around the sides. Let cool to room temperature before serving.

Maple Apple Crumble

MAKES 8 SERVINGS

This crumble is one of the best comfort foods I've ever tasted. My kids give it "Two thumbs up, and two big toes up!" As an added bonus, it's made with fresh fruit, no refined sugar, and protein-rich, fiber-rich quinoa flakes. We eat this for breakfast, at teatime, as dessert, and any time in between.

6 firm tart apples (such as Granny Smith)
1/4 cup raisins
2 tablespoons freshly squeezed lemon juice
1/2 cup maple syrup
3/4 teaspoon ground cinnamon
2 tablespoons cornstarch
11/4 cups Basic Gluten-Free Flour Mix (page 19)

1/4 teaspoon xanthan gum
1 cup quinoa flakes
3/4 cup maple sugar, Sucanat, or firmly packed brown sugar
3/4 cup dairy-free, soy-free vegetable shortening

1. Preheat the oven to 350°F. Grease an 8 by 8-inch or 11 by 7-inch baking dish.

2. Peel and core the apples, cut into bite-size pieces, and place in a large bowl. Toss in the raisins and lemon juice. Add the maple syrup, toss gently, then sprinkle in 1/2 teaspoon of the cinnamon and the cornstarch, stirring gently to combine. Pour into the baking dish, distributing evenly.

3. Combine the flour mix, xanthan gum, quinoa flakes, remaining 1/4 teaspoon cinnamon, and maple sugar.

4. Melt the shortening (about 30 seconds in the microwave does it) and drizzle into the flour mixture, stirring gently to combine until the consistency of a course granola (not paste). Spread the crumble topping evenly over the fruit.

5. Bake in the center of the oven for 35 to 40 minutes, or until the fruit is bubbling up around the sides and the top is golden. Let rest for about 30 minutes before serving.

Blackberry Cobbler

MAKES 8 SERVINGS

Blackberries are so tasty, and so good for you! Packed full of fiber and antioxidants, they are definitely a "superfood." This dessert is tart and sweet. If you like it more tart, add another tablespoon of lime juice.

Blackberry Filling

6 cups fresh blackberries

1 cup granulated sugar

2 tablespoons cornstarch

2 tablespoons freshly squeezed lime juice

Cobbler Biscuit Dough

1 cup Basic Gluten-Free Flour Mix (page 19)

1/4 teaspoon xanthan gum

1 1/2 teaspoons double-acting baking powder

2 tablespoons granulated sugar

1/4 teaspoon salt

1/2 cup dairy-free, soy-free vegetable shortening, chilled and cut into 1/2-inch dice

1/2 cup vanilla vegan yogurt

1 tablespoon dairy-free, soy-free vegetable shortening, for dotting top

1 tablespoon granulated sugar, for sprinkling

1. To make the filling, combine the blackberries, sugar, cornstarch, and lime juice. Toss gently and let rest for about 15 minutes.

2. Preheat the oven to 375°F. Grease an 11 by 7-inch or 8 by 8-inch baking dish.

3. To make the biscuit dough, whisk together the flour mix, xanthan gum, baking powder, sugar, and salt. Add the chilled shortening. Use a pastry blender or two knives to cut it into a coarse meal. Add the vegan yogurt and stir, being sure to incorporate any crumbs at the bottom of the bowl.

4. Pour the blackberries into the baking dish. Dot the top of the berries with the shortening.

5. Use a tablespoon to scoop out the dough onto the fruit. You can also use your fingers to just break it up. Sprinkle with the sugar.

6. Bake for 45 minutes, or until the fruit is bubbling up and the top is golden brown. Let rest for about 30 minutes before serving.

Bourbon Peach Cobbler

MAKES 8 SERVINGS

This recipe is a tribute to my Southern grandmother Catherene, who taught me to bake starting at the tender age of three. Part of her family hailed from Georgia and the others from Kentucky. The peaches are for Georgia, and the bourbon is, of course, for Kentucky!

6 ripe peaches, blanched, peeled, and cut into 12 slices each (see page 138 for blanching tips)

2 tablespoons bourbon

1 teaspoon pure vanilla extract

1/2 teaspoon ground cinnamon

1/2 cup firmly packed light brown sugar

2 tablespoons Basic Gluten-Free Flour Mix (page 19)

1 recipe Cobbler Biscuit Dough (page 149)

1 tablespoon dairy-free, soy-free vegetable shortening, for dotting top

1 tablespoon light brown sugar mixed with 1/8 teaspoon ground cinnamon, for sprinkling

1. Preheat the oven to 375°F. Grease an 11 by 7-inch or 8 by 8-inch baking dish.

2. In a large bowl, combine the peaches, bourbon, vanilla, cinnamon, sugar, and flour mix. Stir to coat the peaches evenly.

3. Prepare the Cobbler Biscuit Dough.

4. Pour the peaches into the baking dish. Dot the top of the peaches with the shortening.

5. Use a tablespoon to scoop out the dough onto the fruit. You can also use your fingers to just break it up. Sprinkle the top with the light brown sugar/cinnamon mixture.

6. Bake for 40 to 45 minutes, or until the fruit is bubbling up and the top is golden brown. Let rest for about 30 minutes before serving.

Banana Bread Pudding

MAKES 8 SERVINGS

Gluten-free bread was made for bread pudding, which is best made with stale bread, because store-bought gluten-free bread is basically stale to begin with (yes, I said it, but you know you've always thought it, too!). To make it even staler, I usually cut it into pieces and lay it out on a baking sheet overnight before making this recipe. Humble, homely, but oh so divine!

3 tablespoons canola oil

1/2 cup Sucanat or brown sugar

2 cups rice milk

1/2 teaspoon ground cinnamon

1/8 teaspoon ground nutmeg

2 teaspoons pure vanilla extract

10 slices gluten-free bread, cut into 1-inch cubes (6 cups)

1/4 teaspoon salt

2 tablespoons flaxseed meal combined with 6 tablespoons hot water ("flax eggs")

3 bananas, sliced into rounds

1/4 cup Sucanat or brown sugar mixed with 1/2 teaspoon ground cinnamon, for sprinkling on top

2 tablespoons dairy-free, soy-free vegetable shortening

1. Combine the canola oil and Sucanat in a heavy saucepan, and cook, stirring, over low heat, for about 3 minutes. Add the rice milk and stir well to combine. Add the cinnamon, nutmeg, and vanilla. Whisk well. Heat over medium-high heat, stirring often, until it begins to boil. Remove from the heat. Pour over the bread cubes in a shallow bowl, toss gently, and let soak for 30 minutes.

2. Preheat the oven to 350°F. Grease an 11 by 7-inch or 8 by 8-inch baking dish with vegetable shortening. Add the salt and "flax eggs" to the bread mixture, stirring gently to combine.

3. Pour half of the bread mixture into the pan. Top with two-thirds of the banana slices. Cover with the remaining half of the bread mixture. Top with the remaining third of the sliced bananas. Sprinkle the Sucanat/cinnamon mixture evenly over the top. Dot with the shortening.

4. Bake for 1 hour, or until caramelized and golden brown on top. Let cool before serving.

Apple Brown Betty

MAKES 8 SERVINGS

Supposedly dating back to Colonial America, this old-fashioned dessert passes the test of time. For a modern spin, try it with a cool glass of rice or hemp milk, and watch for the smiles.

Apple Filling

6 Granny Smith, Crispin, Golden Delicious, or other firm baking apples

1 tablespoon plus 1 1/2 teaspoons Basic Gluten-Free Flour Mix (page 19)

1/4 cup firmly packed brown sugar

1/2 teaspoon ground cinnamon

1/8 teaspoon salt

Crumb

1/2 cup firmly packed light brown sugar

1/2 teaspoon lemon zest

1/2 teaspoon ground cinnamon

Pinch of salt

5 slices gluten-free bread (4 ounces), roughly torn (I use Ener-G Seattle Brown Loaf for this; see Resources, page 177)

2 tablespoons dairy-free, soy-free vegetable shortening

1. Preheat the oven to 375°F. Grease an 8 by 8-inch baking dish liberally with vegetable shortening.

2. To make the filling, peel, core, and slice the apples into 1/4-inch-thick slices. Toss with the flour mix, brown sugar, cinnamon, and salt in a large microwave-safe bowl.

3. Cook the apples in the microwave on high for 6 minutes, stopping to toss gently after 3 minutes, until the syrup is thick and glossy. Remove from the microwave and set aside.

4. To make the crumb, combine the light brown sugar, lemon zest, cinnamon, and salt in a food processor. Pulse to combine.

5. Add the bread and pulse until you have a rough crumb (about 20 pulses).

6. Spread half of the bread crumb mixture in the bottom of the baking dish. Top with the filling, then with the remaining half of the bread crumb mixture. Dot the top with the shortening.

7. Bake in the center of the oven for 40 minutes, or until the top is golden brown and the fruit is bubbling, rotating the pan halfway through. Serve warm or at room temperature. Store, covered, at room temperature.

Tip ▪ Precooking the apples in the microwave is a tip I learned from one of my favorite magazines, *Cook's Illustrated*. What this does is convert the pectin within the apple cells into a more heat-stable form, so you can cook the apples longer without winding up with a soggy mess. In this particular recipe, this provides the extra cooking time the apples need, without causing you to burn the crumb topping. The finished product makes for a betty with a baked, not-too-mushy, not-too-soupy apple filling and a crispy, crunchy crust.

Mango Betty

MAKES 8 SERVINGS

This is perhaps the simplest dessert in this cookbook, and it's also one of the tastiest. It's extremely low in fat and full of good-for-you fruit. I make it when they're selling cut-up mangoes on the cheap at Trader Joe's.

1/2 cup firmly packed light brown sugar
1/2 teaspoon lemon zest
1/2 teaspoon ground cinnamon
1/4 teaspoon ground ginger
1/8 teaspoon ground nutmeg
Pinch of ground cloves
Pinch of salt

5 slices white gluten-free bread (4 ounces), roughly torn (I use Ener-G Tapioca Loaf Thin Sliced for this; see Resources, page 177)
1 1/2 pounds partly ripe mango chunks, cut into 3/4-inch pieces (about 4 1/2 cups)
2 tablespoons freshly squeezed lemon juice
2 tablespoons dairy-free, soy-free vegetable shortening

1. Preheat the oven to 375°F. Grease an 8 by 8-inch baking dish liberally with vegetable shortening.

2. Combine the light brown sugar, lemon zest, cinnamon, ginger, nutmeg, cloves, and salt in a food processor. Pulse to combine.

3. Add the bread and pulse until you have a rough crumb (about 20 pulses).

4. Spread half of the bread crumb mixture in the bottom of the baking dish. Top with the mangoes, sprinkle the mangoes with the lemon juice, and then top with the remaining half of the bread crumb mixture. Dot top with the shortening.

5. Bake in the center of the oven for 45 to 50 minutes, or until the top is golden brown and the fruit is bubbling, rotating the pan halfway through. Serve warm or at room temperature. Store, covered, at room temperature (don't cover it until it's cooled completely or the crumb will get soggy). It's just as good on day two!

Cherry Buckle

MAKES 8 SERVINGS

Buckles differ from crumbles and crisps in that the fruit is interwoven with cake batter, then topped with a crumb topping. This dessert is a favorite of my son Monte's. He loves it for its funny-sounding name and its supreme yumminess. The top should have a buckled or crumpled appearance.

Crumb Topping

1/2 cup firmly packed brown sugar

1/3 cup Basic Gluten-Free Flour Mix (page 19)

1/2 teaspoon ground cinnamon

3 tablespoons dairy-free, soy-free vegetable shortening, chilled and cut into 1/2-inch dice

Buckle

1 pound frozen pitted, sweet dark cherries (about 3 cups), defrosted for 30 minutes, then liquid poured off

13/4 cups plus 2 tablespoons Basic Gluten-Free Flour Mix (page 19)

1/2 teaspoon xanthan gum

2 teaspoons double-acting baking powder

1/2 teaspoon salt

1/2 teaspoon ground cinnamon

1/2 cup dairy-free, soy-free vegetable shortening

3/4 cup granulated sugar

11/2 teaspoons Ener-G egg replacer mixed with 2 tablespoons rice milk

1/2 cup rice milk

1 teaspoon pure vanilla extract

1. Preheat the oven to 350°F. Grease an 8 by 8-inch baking dish liberally with vegetable shortening and sprinkle with a little gluten-free flour mix, tapping out the extra.

2. To make the crumb topping, combine the brown sugar, flour mix, and cinnamon. Add the chilled shortening and work in, using your fingers, until you have a pea-sized crumb. Set aside.

3. To make the buckle, combine the cherries with 2 tablespoons of the flour mix, tossing to coat, and set aside.

4. Whisk together the remaining 13/4 cups flour mix, xanthan gum, baking powder, salt, and cinnamon. Set aside.

5. In the bowl of a stand mixer fitted with the paddle attachment, combine the shortening and granulated sugar on medium speed, beating until light and fluffy, about 2 minutes. Add the egg replacer and mix well, about 1 minute.

6. In a separate bowl, combine the rice milk and vanilla.

7. With the mixer set on low speed, add the flour mixture in three batches, alternating with the rice milk mixture, and beginning and ending with the flour mixture. Fold in the cherries. The batter will be thick.

8. Spoon the batter into the baking dish and sprinkle with the topping.

9. Bake in the center of the oven 55 to 60 minutes, or until the top is deeply golden, rotating the pan halfway through. Let cool to warm or room temperature. Serve unadorned or with Vegan Whipped Topping (page 113) or Vanilla Rice Dream. Store covered. To serve leftovers, rewarm in a 350°F oven for about 15 minutes.

Rustic Moroccan Loaves (page 165)
and Focaccia (page 168)

7

YEASTED BAKED GOODS
and Savories

What makes gluten-free breadmaking so special, aside from the opportunity to use fiber-packed and nutrient-rich old-world grains such as millet and sorghum? Well, for starters, you don't have to knead gluten-free bread dough, and it only requires one rise because I use rapid-rise yeast (also known as quick-rise yeast, fast-rising yeast, instant yeast, and/or bread machine yeast) instead of traditional baker's yeast. Wow, that's a time-saver! Who knew that dietary restrictions could actually simplify your life?

Okay, okay, but you're still baking your own bread. "That's not as simple as shopping for it," you protest. But here's the rub. Most store-bought gluten-free bread is hard as a rock, and often frozen to boot. Ener-G makes some wonderful soft and very tasty gluten-free sliced bread, but you usually have to order it directly from Ener-G. I am particularly fond of their Seattle Brown Loaf, which is made with montina flour, an amazing high-protein, high-fiber grain from Montana (of course).

But what's a gluten-free person to do when she doesn't have any Ener-G? Bake some up, I say! Why go spend a thousand dollars on Whole Foods' gluten-free rocks

CONTINUED

(which by the way, often contain dairy, eggs, and soy) when you can make your own tasty, artisanal, allergen-free breads from scratch? I've provided recipes that will make good bread for slicing for toast; bread for sandwiches; bread for accompanying soups, salads, and dips; pizza crust; flat breads; and most versatile of all, the continental roll. This takes us full circle, I guess, because I started the book with breakfast goods.

Gluten-Free Bread Flour Mix

MAKES 6 CUPS

1 1/2 cups millet flour
1 1/2 cups sorghum flour

2 cups tapioca starch
1 cup potato starch

1. To measure flour, use a large spoon to scoop flour into the measuring cup, then level it off with the back of a knife or straightedge. Do *not* use the measuring cup itself to scoop your flour when measuring! It will compact the flour and you will wind up with too much for the recipe.

2. Combine all of the ingredients in a gallon-size zipper-top bag. Shake until well blended. Store in the refrigerator until ready to use.

Note ■ For recipes in this chapter, be careful not to overheat liquids before combining them with the yeast. If the liquids are too hot, they will kill the yeast—and the rise. Invest in a thermometer and stick to the temperature recommendations firmly.

Potato Bread

MAKES 1 9 BY 5-INCH LOAF

This is classic slicing bread, great for toast in the morning, and wonderful for sandwiches. Make it the morning after a big supper when you have leftover mashed or baked potatoes.

1¼ cups warm water (110° to 115°F)

⅓ cup plus 1 tablespoon firmly packed light brown sugar

1 (¼-ounce) packet rapid-rise yeast

3½ cups Gluten-Free Bread Flour Mix (page 158)

½ cup millet flour

1 tablespoon xanthan gum

¼ teaspoon ground cardamom

1 cup mashed potatoes

2 teaspoons salt

⅓ cup dairy-free, soy-free vegetable shortening, plus 1 tablespoon for brushing top of loaf

⅓ cup Better Than Milk rice milk powder or other vegan milk powder

1½ teaspoons Ener-G egg replacer mixed with 2 tablespoons room temperature rice milk

1. Combine ¼ cup of the warm water, 1 tablespoon of the light brown sugar, and the yeast in the bowl of a stand mixer fitted with the paddle attachment (not bread hook). Use a wooden spoon or whisk to mix well. Make sure the yeast is completely dissolved.

2. Whisk together the flour mix, millet flour, xanthan gum, and cardamom. Set aside.

3. In a pan, combine the mashed potatoes, remaining 1 cup water, salt, ⅓ cup of the vegetable shortening, rice milk powder, and remaining ⅓ cup light brown sugar. Mix well. Heat until warm and the shortening has melted. Let come to 110° to 115°F.

4. Add the egg replacer to the yeast mixture, stirring well. Add the potato mixture to the yeast mixture and beat on medium speed until combined, about 1 minute.

5. Add the flour mixture to the liquid mixture in two batches, mixing well on medium speed for about 1 minute, until the dough is fully combined.

6. Grease a 9 by 5-inch loaf pan liberally with vegetable shortening.

7. Use a rubber spatula to turn the dough out onto a well-floured board, flour your hands well, and pat the dough into a disk 7 inches in diameter and 1½ inches thick. Flip, and then pat into a rectangle about 11 inches long and 1½ inches thick. Roll up, starting from the longer edge, and seal the seam tightly, pressing down lightly to press out any trapped air pockets. Make sure the seam is on the bottom. Tuck both ends of the loaf under (against the seam), so the dough will fit in the loaf pan. The dough will be soft, but don't worry, it's supposed to be. Transfer to the loaf pan. Melt the remaining 1 tablespoon shortening (about 30 seconds in the microwave should do it) and use a pastry brush to coat the top of the loaf. Cover with a folded clean dish towel or cloth napkin.

CONTINUED

Place the loaf pan in a dishpan and pour hot water to come two-thirds up the sides of the loaf (or just fill your kitchen sink basin). Be sure to fold your cloth so it's not dragging in the water. Let the loaf rise for 1 hour. I generally replace the hot water with new hot water after the first 30 minutes. Check it periodically to make sure it's still quite warm.

8. After the dough has risen for 1 hour and has about doubled in size, place the loaf in a cold oven. Set the temperature to 400°F and bake for 20 minutes. Reduce the temperature to 325°F and bake for 40 minutes longer, or until the loaf is deeply golden on top. Transfer to a cooling rack, turn out of the pan, and let cool (if you can wait that long!).

Tip ■ Contrary to popular belief, bread products actually dry out faster in the fridge. When storing your gluten-free breads, let them cool completely, then wrap them tightly in foil, plastic wrap, or a freezer bag (with the extra air squeezed out) and store them at room temperature, preferably in a bread box. To crisp up your crust again, just reheat the bread in a 350°F oven for about 15 minutes until warmed through. Or slice and toast individual slices. You may also store your breads in the freezer for up to 3 months. Just remove from the freezer, let defrost to room temperature, and rewarm in the oven as directed above.

"Buttermilk" Raisin Bread

MAKES 1 9 BY 5-INCH LOAF

This majestic brown bread is an excellent breakfast loaf. Try it toasted with a little vegan margarine. If truth be told, this is my favorite meal of the day.

1½ cups rice milk

1 tablespoon plus 1½ teaspoons freshly squeezed lemon juice

¼ cup warm water (110° to 115°F)

¼ cup molasses

1 (¼-ounce) packet rapid-rise yeast

3 tablespoons dairy-free, soy-free vegetable shortening, plus 1 tablespoon for brushing top of loaf

5 cups Gluten-Free Bread Flour Mix (page 158)

1 tablespoon xanthan gum

2 teaspoons salt

½ teaspoon baking soda

½ cup raisins

1. Combine the rice milk and lemon juice and set aside to sour into "buttermilk" for 30 minutes.

2. Combine the warm water, molasses, and yeast in the bowl of a stand mixer fitted with the paddle attachment (not bread hook). Use a wooden spoon or whisk to mix well. Make sure the yeast is completely dissolved.

3. Add 3 tablespoons of the shortening to the soured rice milk, and heat until the shortening melts. Let come to 110° to 115°F, then add to the yeast mixture, stirring well to combine.

4. Whisk together the flour mix, xanthan gum, salt, and baking soda. Stir in the raisins.

5. Add the flour mixture to the liquid mixture in two batches, mixing well on medium speed for about 1 minute, or until the dough is fully combined.

6. Grease a 9 by 5-inch loaf pan liberally with vegetable shortening.

7. Use a rubber spatula to turn the dough out onto a well-floured board, flour your hands well, and pat the dough into a disk 7 inches in diameter and 1½ inches thick. Flip, and then pat into a rectangle about 11 inches long and 1½ inches thick. Roll up, starting from the longer edge, and seal the seam tightly, pressing down lightly to press out any trapped air pockets. Make sure the seam is on the bottom. Tuck both ends of the loaf under (against the seam), so the dough will fit in the loaf pan. The dough will be soft and sticky, but don't worry, it's supposed to be. Transfer to the loaf pan. Melt the remaining 1 tablespoon shortening (about 30 seconds in the microwave should do it) and use a pastry brush to coat the top of the loaf. Cover with a folded clean dish towel or cloth napkin. Place the loaf pan in a dishpan and pour hot water to come two-thirds up the

CONTINUED

sides of the loaf (or just fill your kitchen sink basin). Be sure to fold your cloth so it's not dragging in the water. Let the loaf rise for 1 hour. I generally replace the hot water with new hot water after the first 30 minutes. Check it periodically to make sure it's still quite warm.

8. After the dough has risen for 1 hour and has about doubled in size, place the loaf in a cold oven. Set the temperature to 400°F and bake for 20 minutes. Reduce the temperature to 325°F and bake for 40 minutes longer, or until the loaf is deeply browned on top. Transfer to a cooling rack, turn out of the pan, and let cool (if you can wait that long . . . I can't with this one!).

Buckwheat and Corn Bread

MAKES 1 9 BY 5-INCH LOAF

This hearty old-world bread is great eaten anywhere you'd traditionally eat rye or pumpernickel bread. Use maple syrup to make it like "rye" or molasses for "pumpernickel."

1½ cups rice milk

1 tablespoon cider vinegar

¼ cup warm water (110° to 115°F)

¼ cup maple syrup or molasses

1 (¼-ounce) packet rapid-rise yeast

2 tablespoons canola oil

2 cups Gluten-Free Bread Flour Mix (page 158)

1½ cups buckwheat flour

1 cup cornmeal

1 tablespoon xanthan gum

2 teaspoons salt

½ teaspoon baking soda

2 teaspoons caraway seeds

1. In a small bowl, combine the rice milk and cider vinegar and set aside.

2. Combine the warm water, maple syrup, and yeast in the bowl of a stand mixer fitted with the paddle attachment (not bread hook). Use a wooden spoon or whisk to mix well. Make sure the yeast is completely dissolved.

3. Heat the rice milk mixture to 110° to 115°F, add the canola oil, and then add to the yeast mixture, stirring well to combine.

4. Whisk together the flour mix, buckwheat flour, cornmeal, xanthan gum, salt, baking soda, and caraway seeds.

5. Add the flour mixture to the liquid mixture in two batches, mixing well on medium speed for about 1 minute, or until the dough is fully combined.

6. Spray a 9 by 5-inch loaf pan liberally with baking spray, or grease with vegetable shortening or canola oil.

7. Use a rubber spatula to turn the dough out onto a well-floured board (add a little cornmeal, too), flour your hands well, and pat the dough into a disk 7 inches in diameter and 1½ inches thick. Flip, and then pat into a rectangle about 11 inches long and 1½ inches thick. Roll up, starting from the longer edge, and seal the seam tightly, pressing down lightly to press out any trapped air pockets. Make sure the seam is on the bottom. Tuck both ends of the loaf under (against the seam), so the dough will fit in the loaf pan. Transfer to the loaf pan. Spray the top of loaf liberally with baking spray (or brush with 1 tablespoon melted vegetable shortening or canola oil). Cover with a folded clean dish towel or cloth napkin. Place the loaf pan in a dishpan and pour hot water to come two-thirds up the sides (or just fill your kitchen sink basin). Be sure to fold your cloth so it's not dragging in the water. Let the loaf rise for 1 hour. I generally replace the hot water with new hot water after the first 30 minutes. Check it periodically to make sure it's still quite warm.

CONTINUED

8. After the dough has risen for 1 hour and has about doubled in size, place the loaf in a cold oven. Set the temperature to 400°F and bake for 20 minutes. Reduce the temperature to 325°F and bake for 35 minutes longer, or until the loaf is deeply browned on top. Transfer to a cooling rack, turn out of the pan, and let cool for at least 15 minutes before slicing.

Gluten-Free-Beer Bread

MAKES 1 9 BY 5-INCH LOAF

The easiest loaf of bread you'll ever bake, ever. The yeast in the beer eliminates the need for a rise with traditional yeast. So thank you, whoever you are, for the advent of gluten-free beer . . . for so many reasons. For those of you making this for children, I can hear you now, but do not fear, the alcohol cooks out, just leaving behind a wonderfully subtle yeasty beer flavor. I use Redbridge, made by Anheuser-Busch (yes, they make Budweiser!), because it's easy to find, but if you want to use a gluten-free microbrewery beer, bake your socks off. This bread is fantastic with soup or salad, or really anything savory.

3 cups Gluten-Free Bread Flour Mix (page 158)
2 teaspoons xanthan gum
1 (12-ounce) bottle gluten-free beer
2 tablespoons light agave nectar

1 tablespoon double-acting baking powder
1 teaspoon salt
3 tablespoons dairy-free, soy-free vegetable shortening

1. Preheat the oven to 375°F. Grease a 9 by 5-inch loaf pan liberally with vegetable shortening.

2. Combine the flour mix and xanthan gum in a large bowl. Whisk well. Add the beer and agave nectar and mix well to combine, about 1 minute. Let rest until the oven is heated.

3. Just prior to baking, add the baking powder and salt. Mix vigorously, scraping the bottom of the bowl.

4. Transfer the dough to the loaf pan. Smooth down the top with a frosting spatula. Melt 2 tablespoons of the shortening, about 1 minute in the microwave. Brush over the top of the loaf using a pastry brush.

5. Bake the bread in the center of the oven for 30 minutes. Remove from the oven, brush the top liberally with the remaining 1 tablespoon shortening, rotate the pan, and bake for 30 minutes longer, or until deeply golden and the bread sounds hollow when rapped on top. Transfer to a cooling rack. Let rest in the pan for 5 minutes. Turn out of the pan and let cool for about 15 minutes before slicing with a serrated knife.

Rustic Moroccan Loaves

MAKES 2 ROUND 7-INCH LOAVES

This simple no-knead bread is so easy, you could make it every day. It's great for scooping or dipping; just break off a chunk and dig in.

1¼ cups warm water (110° to 115°F)
2 tablespoons light agave nectar
1 (¼-ounce) packet rapid-rise yeast
3½ cups Gluten-Free Bread Flour Mix
   (page 158)

2 teaspoons xanthan gum
1 teaspoon salt
2 tablespoons olive oil

1. Combine the warm water, agave nectar, and yeast in the bowl of a stand mixer fitted with the paddle attachment (not bread hook). Use a wooden spoon or whisk to mix well. Make sure the yeast is completely dissolved.

2. Whisk together the flour mix, xanthan gum, and salt. Add to the yeast mixture in two batches, mixing on medium speed, until the dough is fully combined, about 1 minute.

3. Dust a baking sheet liberally with flour mix, flour your hands, and divide the dough into two balls. Place the balls on the baking sheet and shape them into two 5-inch dome-shaped loaves.

4. Brush the tops with 1 tablespoon of the olive oil using a pastry brush. Cover with a light dish towel or plastic wrap (but don't wrap it tightly, or you'll inhibit the rise) and let rise in a warm place (85°F) free from drafts. I like to place it in an unheated oven with a pan of hot water placed on the bottom of the oven. If it's a warm day, this won't be necessary. The top of the fridge is good, too. Let rise for 1 hour, or until you can push a finger in to one knuckle deep and the indent remains.

5. In the last 20 minutes of your rise, preheat the oven to 350°F. (Remove the bread and pan of water if the loaves are rising in the oven and let them finish their rise somewhere else.)

6. Uncover the loaves and use a sharp knife to cut a ½-inch deep cross in the top of each loaf. Brush the loaves with the remaining 1 tablespoon olive oil and bake for 15 minutes. Remove from the oven and brush the tops of the loaves with water. Return to the oven and bake for 15 minutes longer, or until the bread sounds hollow when rapped on the bottom. It will not brown, so don't use that as your judge. Let cool slightly on cooling racks. Break apart or slice with a serrated knife.

Seeded Boule

MAKES 1 ROUND 10-INCH LOAF

This is an outstanding loaf of bread and a great way to showcase your talents as an allergen-free baker. I have chosen seeds that I know can be found free of cross-contamination risk with other allergens (see Resources, page 177), but feel free to substitute.

1 1/2 cups rice milk

1 tablespoon plus 1 1/2 teaspoons freshly squeezed lemon juice

1/4 cup warm water (110° to 115°F)

1/4 cup light agave nectar

1 (1/4-ounce) packet rapid-rise yeast

3 tablespoons dairy-free, soy-free vegetable shortening, plus 1 tablespoon for brushing top of loaf

5 cups Gluten-Free Bread Flour Mix (page 158)

1 tablespoon xanthan gum

2 teaspoons salt

1/2 teaspoon baking soda

1/4 cup sunflower seeds, plus 2 tablespoons for sprinkling on top of loaf

2 tablespoons flaxseeds, plus 1 teaspoon for sprinkling on top of loaf

1 tablespoon poppy seeds, plus 1/2 teaspoon for sprinkling on top of loaf

1. In a small bowl, combine the rice milk and lemon juice and set aside.

2. Combine the warm water, agave nectar, and yeast in the bowl of a stand mixer fitted with the paddle attachment (not bread hook). Use a wooden spoon or whisk to mix well. Make sure the yeast is completely dissolved.

3. Add 3 tablespoons of the shortening to the rice milk, and heat until the shortening melts. Let come to 110° to 115°F, then add to the yeast mixture, stirring well to combine.

4. Whisk together the flour mix, xanthan gum, salt, and baking soda. Stir in the seeds for the dough, reserving the seeds for sprinkling.

5. Add the flour mixture to the liquid mixture in two batches, mixing well on medium speed for about 1 minute, or until the dough is fully combined. It will be wet and sticky. If it is too wet, add a little more flour mix, 1 tablespoon at a time, but the lighter the dough, the lighter the bread will be.

6. Dust a baking sheet liberally with cornmeal.

7. Use a rubber spatula to transfer the dough to a well-floured board. Sprinkle the top of the dough with a little more flour mix, flip the dough, and shape into a ball. Transfer to the baking sheet and mold into a dome-shaped loaf about 7 inches in diameter.

8. Melt the remaining 1 tablespoon shortening (about 1 minute in the microwave does it) and brush over the top of the loaf using a pastry brush. Cover with a folded clean dish towel or cloth napkin. Place a pan of very hot water in the bottom of the oven. Put the

baking sheet with the bread in the oven, with the oven turned off. Let the loaf rise for 1 hour.

9. After the dough has risen for 1 hour, remove from the oven, refill the pan of water with new hot water (this will create steam, which gives you that coveted crunchy crust), and preheat the oven to 400°F. Brush the top of the loaf gently with cold water and sprinkle with the remaining seeds. Bake for 15 minutes, remove from the oven, spray or brush lightly with more cold water, return to the oven, and bake for 25 minutes longer, or until the loaf is golden on top. Transfer the loaf from the baking sheet to a cooling rack and let cool.

Focaccia

MAKES 1 SQUARE 9-INCH BREAD

This rustic flat bread is great served with white bean dip or dunked in red sauce. It's also wonderful dipped in olive oil. Be sure to serve it warm.

1½ cups warm water (110° to 115°F)
1 teaspoon agave nectar or granulated sugar
1 (¼-ounce) packet rapid-rise yeast
3½ cups Gluten-Free Bread Flour Mix
   (page 158)

1 tablespoon xanthan gum
1 tablespoon salt
¼ cup olive oil
1½ teaspoons coarse sea salt
1½ teaspoons chopped fresh rosemary

1. Combine the water, agave nectar, and yeast in a large bowl. Mix well. Make sure the yeast is completely dissolved.

2. Whisk together the flour mix, xanthan gum, and salt.

3. Add the flour mixture to the yeast mixture in two batches and mix well for about 1 minute, or until the dough is coming together.

4. Spray a 9 by 9-inch baking pan with baking spray or grease with vegetable shortening and dust with cornmeal, tapping out any extra.

5. Transfer the dough to the pan, using a rubber spatula. Use a frosting spatula to smooth down the surface and coax the dough into the corners of the pan. Cover with a folded dish towel or cloth napkin. Place the pan in a dishpan and pour hot water to come two-thirds up the sides (or just fill your kitchen sink basin). It may float, but don't worry, that's fine. Be sure to fold your cloth so it's not dragging in the water. Let the bread rise for 1 hour. I generally replace the hot water with new hot water after the first 30 minutes. Check it periodically to make sure it's still quite warm.

6. After the dough has risen for 1 hour, use your fingers to gently make dimples all over the top of the bread. Return the bread to its warm bath to continue rising while you preheat the oven.

7. Preheat the oven to 450°F. Once it's heated, pour the olive oil over the top of the bread, brushing lightly with a pastry brush to distribute it evenly. Sprinkle the top with the coarse sea salt and rosemary. Bake for about 22 minutes, or until golden on top. Transfer to a cooling rack, turn out of the pan, and let cool for about 15 minutes before slicing.

Pizza Crust

MAKES 1 18 BY 13-INCH RECTANGULAR CRUST, 2 9-INCH ROUND CRUSTS,
OR 2 12-INCH THIN ROUND CRUSTS

My son Lennon is a pizza fanatic. He calls this crust "awesome!" High praise indeed for such an easy-peezy pizza pie. Top this crust with tomato sauce, onions, sliced mushrooms, sliced tomatoes, basil, and any other veggie you desire. The possibilities are endless.

1¼ cups warm water (110° to 115°F)
1 teaspoon agave nectar or granulated sugar
1 (¼-ounce) packet rapid-rise yeast
3 tablespoons olive oil

3 cups Gluten-Free Bread Flour Mix (page 158)
½ cup millet flour
3½ teaspoons xanthan gum
1 teaspoon salt

1. Combine the warm water, agave nectar, and yeast in the bowl of a stand mixer fitted with the paddle attachment (not bread hook). Use a wooden spoon or whisk to mix well. Add 1 tablespoon of the olive oil and stir well. Make sure the yeast is completely dissolved.

2. Whisk together the flour mix, millet flour, xanthan gum, and salt.

3. Add the flour mixture to the yeast mixture and mix well for about 1 minute, or until the dough is coming together.

4. Sprinkle an 18 by 13-inch baking sheet, two 9-inch round pizza pans, or two 12-inch pizza pans with cornmeal. Flour a board well with flour mix.

5. Using a rubber spatula, transfer the dough to the board. Sprinkle a little flour mix on top of the dough, flour a rolling pin, and roll the dough out into a rectangle large enough to fit the baking sheet, or into two circles. Transfer the dough to the pan or pans (I use a large metal spatula to assist in this), pat the dough to the edges, and brush with the remaining 2 tablespoons olive oil, using a pastry brush. Cover with a light dish towel or plastic wrap (but don't wrap it tightly, or you'll inhibit the rise) and let rise in a warm (85°F) place free from drafts. I like to place it in an unheated oven with a pan of hot water placed on the bottom of the oven. If it's a warm day, this won't be necessary. The top of the fridge is good, too. Let rise for 1 hour.

6. Remove the pan of water from the oven. Preheat the oven to 500°F (transfer the dough elsewhere if it's rising in the oven).

7. Flatten the center of the crust with the palm of your hand, leaving a raised edge around the perimeter. Top with whatever topping you like, and bake for 15 minutes, or until the crust is golden and the topping has cooked.

8. Let cool slightly before eating. This baby is hot!

Socca de Nice

MAKES 4 10-INCH SOCCAS

I first became interested in soccas (chickpea flour crepes) because they are allergen-free, gluten-free, low-carb, high-protein, and delicious! Soccas go back to at least 1860. They are from southern France, but were most likely an import from northern Africa, where they eat a lot of chickpeas. In the nineteenth century, there were socca sellers at the markets and at work sites, where they provided the morning meal to the workers. The socca sellers used special wagons with built-in charcoal ovens to keep their wares hot while they announced them with the appropriate cries of "Socca! Socca! Socca!" I have kept my socca recipe simple, because I like the rustic flavor. You can top it with olive oil, salt, and fresh pepper, or go all out, topping it with things like caramelized onions and grilled red peppers.

1 1/2 cups cold water

3 tablespoons olive oil

1 teaspoon kosher salt

2 cups chickpea flour (also called garbanzo bean flour, gram flour, cici flour, chana flour, or besan flour)

1/2 teaspoon cumin

Super canola oil or other high-heat cooking oil, such as super safflower or avocado oil

1. Preheat the oven to 550°F.

2. In a large bowl, whisk together the water, olive oil, and salt. Add the chickpea flour, a little at a time, whisking it in completely. Stir in the cumin. Whisk for about 1 minute. You want this batter smooth! Add a little more water if it seems too thick; you want it thin like crepe batter. Once you've whisked it so it has absolutely no lumps, set aside.

3. Preheat a 10-inch cast-iron skillet in the oven, 4 to 5 minutes, then remove (with an oven mitt or pot holder; it's *hot!*). Coat the pan with super canola oil, swirling it around. Then, working quickly, add a heaping 1/2 cup of the batter to the pan, swirling it around to fill the pan in an even layer. Put in the oven and cook for 5 to 7 minutes, until browned a bit around the edges. Remove from the oven. Flip. It should be golden brown on the bottom. Transfer to a plate, add a little more oil to the pan, add another 1/2 cup of batter, and cook, repeating until you've used all the batter. You can cut it into wedges and dip it into olive oil, or drizzle olive oil on top and sprinkle with salt and pepper.

Variations ■ To add herbal flavor, heat 1/2 teaspoon of dried herbs such as rosemary or thyme in the olive oil for 2 minutes over medium heat. Let the olive oil cool before making the recipe. You may also make these on the stove top. I like the texture slightly better in the oven, but the stove top is much quicker. To do so, heat your cast-iron skillet over medium-high heat. Add a little olive oil. Once hot, add the batter. Cook for about 1 minute, flip, and cook for 1 minute more. Remove from the pan.

Matzo

MAKES 2 8-INCH MATZOS

Traditional matzo recipes are made from water and one of the five grains permitted for Passover. These are barley, oats, rye, spelt, and wheat. This creates a problem for the gluten-free Jew. But help is on the horizon. This matzo is not made from grain at all; it's made from potato starch and flaxseed meal, and I did adhere to the Passover rule that the matzo be made in eighteen minutes or less.

3/4 cup potato starch

1/4 cup golden flaxseed meal

1/4 teaspoon kosher salt

2 tablespoons dairy-free, soy-free vegetable shortening

1/4 cup water

1. Preheat the oven to 400°F.

2. Combine the potato starch, flaxseed meal, and salt in a bowl. Add the shortening and use a wooden spoon to combine. Add the water, 1 tablespoon at a time. Your dough should be the consistency of Play-Doh. If it's too sticky, add a little more potato starch.

3. Lay out a sheet of parchment paper on your work surface. Transfer the dough and use your hands to combine into a ball. Divide in half, setting half aside. Mold into a ball, cover with another sheet of parchment paper, and roll out into a circle 8 inches in diameter. Peel off the top sheet of parchment paper, and then replace it. Flip the dough, still between the two sheets of parchment paper, and peel off the other sheet of parchment paper. Discard it. Using a fork, prick the matzo about 12 times. Transfer the matzo, still on the parchment paper, to a baking sheet. Trim the excess parchment paper. Repeat with the other half of the dough. You should be able to fit both on the same baking sheet.

4. Bake for 15 minutes, until lightly golden. Transfer to a cooling rack to let cool completely. It will become crisp once it's cooled.

Cornbread Sticks

MAKES 14 BREAD STICKS

My grandmother and mother very often made cornbread sticks along with our summer suppers when I was a child. I grew up on Cape Cod, and we ate a lot of fresh fish back in those days. Cod, haddock, flounder, and bluefish were all staples at our summer table. Cornbread is eaten alongside fish to help push down any bones you might accidentally swallow. Due to food allergies, and tragically polluted and overfished waters, we've stopped eating the fish. But the cornbread sticks have remained. My mother still bakes them up every year when we go back East for our annual summer reunions, and I make them for my kids, who love them just as much as I always have. I make them with my Basic Gluten-Free Flour Mix, but you may also use Gluten-Free Bread Flour Mix (page 158) for a more intense flavor and a slightly more crumbly texture.

1 cup rice milk

1 tablespoon freshly squeezed lemon juice

1 cup Basic Gluten-Free Flour Mix (page 19)

1 cup yellow cornmeal

1/2 teaspoon xanthan gum

3/4 teaspoon salt

1 tablespoon double-acting baking powder

1/4 cup granulated sugar

1 1/2 teaspoons Ener-G egg replacer mixed with 2 tablespoons rice milk

1/4 cup dairy-free, soy-free vegetable shortening, melted

1. Preheat the oven to 425°F. Grease two cornstick pans liberally with vegetable shortening (I prefer using this to baking spray, because it remains more stable at high temperatures). Alternately, you may also use a muffin pan, popover pan, or cast-iron skillet.

2. Combine the rice milk and lemon juice. Set aside.

3. Whisk together the flour mix, cornmeal, xanthan gum, salt, baking powder, and sugar in a large bowl.

4. Add the rice milk mixture and stir to combine. Add the egg replacer and melted shortening. Stir a couple of times until smooth. Fill the cornstick molds two-thirds full. Smooth the tops so the batter fills the mold. Bake for about 20 minutes, or until golden. Turn out immediately onto a cooling rack, or better yet, into a bread basket to be passed at the table. Serve warm.

Dinner Rolls

MAKES 24 2-INCH ROLLS

Soft and warm, these rolls have a wonderful aroma. I have given proportions for a large batch because I find these rolls get gobbled up quickly. They also freeze well, so you can keep a batch in the freezer, defrosting, then warming a few . . . whenever.

1¼ cups warm water (110° to 115°F)
⅓ cup plus 1 tablespoon granulated sugar
1 (¼-ounce) packet rapid-rise yeast
4 cups Gluten-Free Bread Flour Mix (page 158)
1 tablespoon xanthan gum
1½ teaspoons salt
1 cup mashed potatoes
⅓ cup dairy-free, soy-free vegetable shortening, melted

⅓ cup Better Than Milk rice milk powder or other vegan milk powder
1½ teaspoons Ener-G egg replacer mixed with 2 tablespoons rice milk, at room temperature
Baking spray, for coating tops of rolls (see Tip, opposite)

1. Combine the warm water, sugar, and yeast in the bowl of a stand mixer fitted with the paddle attachment (not bread hook). Use a wooden spoon or whisk to mix well. Make sure the yeast is completely dissolved.

2. Whisk together the flour mix, xanthan gum, and salt. Set aside.

3. Add the mashed potatoes, melted shortening, and rice milk powder to the yeast mixture. Beat on medium speed for about 1 minute. Add the egg replacer and mix on medium speed until smooth, 1 minute more. Add the flour mixture to the yeast mixture in two batches, and mix well on medium speed, until the dough is coming together, about 1 minute.

4. Grease two 9-inch round cake pans liberally with vegetable shortening.

5. Using a rubber spatula, turn out the dough onto a well-floured board. Sprinkle the top of the dough with flour mix, pat into a disk, and cut in half. Roll the dough into two 12-inch logs. Cut one log into 12 pieces. Roll the pieces vigorously between your hands into 12 smooth balls. Place the balls in the first pan. It's fine if they're touching. Repeat with the remaining log. Spray the rolls with baking spray. Cover the pans with clean dish towels or cloth napkins. Put a pan of very hot water in the bottom of the oven. Place the rolls in the oven and let rise for 1 hour.

6. Remove all of the pans from the oven and preheat the oven to 400°F.

7. Once the oven is preheated, spray the rolls again with baking spray and bake for about 25 minutes, or until golden on top. Remove from the oven. You may spray them once more with baking spray to keep them soft, or leave as is for a slightly harder roll. Serve warm or at room temperature. To freeze, let them cool completely, then store in a gallon-size freezer bag.

Continental Rolls

MAKES 8 3¹/₂-INCH ROLLS

These multipurpose rolls are great as part of a continental breakfast, for making ciabatta sandwiches or panini, along with soup or salad for lunch, and they are a fabulous roll to pass at dinner. This one covers all your bases. Bon appetit!

1¹/₂ cups warm water (110° to 115°F)
1 tablespoon light agave nectar
1 (¹/₄-ounce) packet rapid-rise yeast
4 cups Gluten-Free Bread Flour Mix (page 158)

1 tablespoon xanthan gum
2 teaspoons salt
Baking spray for coating tops of rolls

1. Combine the warm water, agave nectar, and yeast in the bowl of a stand mixer fitted with the paddle attachment (not bread hook). Use a wooden spoon or whisk to mix well. Make sure the yeast is completely dissolved.

2. Whisk together the flour mix, xanthan gum, and salt. Add to the yeast mixture in two batches and beat on medium speed, scraping down the sides of the bowl as necessary, until the dough is combined, about 1 minute.

3. Dust a baking sheet liberally with cornmeal.

4. Use a rubber spatula to turn out the dough onto a well-floured board. Sprinkle the top of the dough with flour mix, pat into a disk, and cut in half. Roll the dough into two 12-inch logs. Cut one log into 4 pieces. Shape into 3 by 3-inch rectangles. Place on the baking sheet. Repeat with the other log. Spray the tops of the rolls with baking spray. Cover the rolls with a clean dish towel or tea towel. Place a pan of very hot water in the bottom of the oven. Put the baking sheet with the rolls in the oven, with the oven turned off. Let rise for 1 hour. In the last 20 minutes of the rise, remove the rolls from the oven, replace the pan of hot water with new hot water (this will create steam, which gives you that coveted crunchy crust), and preheat the oven to 375°F. Let the rolls continue to rise on the counter while the oven is heating. Brush the tops of the rolls gently with cold water. Bake for 15 minutes, remove from the oven, brush the rolls again with cold water, return to the oven, and bake for about 20 minutes longer, or until the rolls are lightly golden on top. Transfer the rolls to a cooling rack and let cool slightly. Serve warm. To reheat, place in a 350°F oven for about 15 minutes, directly on the rack.

Tip ■ Instead of using baking spray, you can also melt 2 tablespoons of vegetable shortening and brush the rolls with it using a pastry brush.

RESOURCES

SAFETY NOTE: Because each person's food sensitivities and reactions are unique, ranging from mild intolerance to life-threatening and severe food allergies, it is up to the consumer to monitor ingredients and manufacturing conditions. If manufacturing conditions, potential cross-contamination between foods, and ingredient derivatives pose a risk for you, please reread all food labels and call the manufacturer to confirm potential allergen concerns *before* consumption. Ingredients and manufacturing practices can change overnight and without warning.

That being said, the following products are, to the best of my knowledge, allergen-free. Look for these products at your local natural foods store or grocery store, or order them online.

Product Brands

Amaranth Flour

Nu-World Amaranth Flour
NU-WORLD FOODS
- www.nuworldamaranth.com

Baking Powder

Clabber Girl
CLABBER GIRL, RUMFORD, AND DAVIS BAKING POWDERS
- www.clabbergirl.com

Brown Rice Flour

Superfine Brown Rice Flour
AUTHENTIC FOODS
- www.glutenfree-supermarket.com
Authentic Foods is my favorite brand of brown rice flour, but please note, though it's processed in a dedicated gluten-free plant, it is not processed in a dedicated nut-free plant—for a dedicated gluten-free and allergen-free brown rice flour, see Ener-G, below.

Brown Rice Flour
ENER-G FOODS
- www.ener-g.com

Buckwheat Flour

ARROWHEAD MILLS
- www.arrowheadmills.com

Canola Oil

CRISCO CANOLA OIL
- www.crisco.com

Chocolate Bars

Boom CHOCO Boom bars
ENJOY LIFE FOODS
- www.enjoylifefoods.com

SCHARFFEN BERGER SEMISWEET AND BITTERSWEET HOME BAKING BARS
- www.scharffenberger.com

Chocolate Chips

Semisweet Chocolate Chips
ENJOY LIFE
■ www.enjoylifefoods.com
These are the easiest AF/GF chips you can find; I'm a huge fan.

Coconut Flavor/Extract, Mint Extract, Etc.

FRONTIER NATURAL PRODUCTS
■ www.frontiercoop.com

Coconut Milk Yogurt

So Delicious Coconut Milk Yogurt
TURTLE MOUNTAIN
■ www.turtlemountain.com

Cornstarch, Organic, GMO-Free

LET'S DO . . . ORGANIC
■ www.edwardandsons.com

Corn Syrup, Organic, GMO-Free

WHOLESOME SWEETENERS
■ www.organicsugars.biz

Dairy-Free, Soy-Free Vegetable Shortening

Spectrum Organic Shortening
SPECTRUM ORGANIC PRODUCTS
■ www.spectrumorganics.com

Date Sugar

NOW FOODS
■ www.nowfoods.com

Decorating Sugar

Nature's Colors Sugar
INDIA TREE
■ www.indiatree.com

Egg Replacer

ENER-G EGG REPLACER
■ www.ener-g.com

Flaxseeds

PREMIUM GOLD FLAX PRODUCTS, INC.
■ www.flaxpremiumgold.com

Food Coloring

Seelect All Natural/Organic Food Coloring
SEELECT
■ www.seelecttea.com

Gluten-Free, Allergen-Free Cereals

Perky O's
Perky's Nutty Flax
Perky's Nutty Rice
■ www.perkysnaturalfoods.com

Gluten-Free Oats

Gluten-Free Oats
■ www.glutenfreeoats.com

Lara's Rolled Oats
CREAM HILL ESTATES
■ www.creamhillestates.com

Hemp Milk

LIVING HARVEST HEMP MILK
■ www.worldpantry.com

Maple Sugar

Authentic Foods Gluten-Free Maple Sugar
AUTHENTIC FOODS
■ www.glutenfree-supermarket.com

Millet Flour

ARROWHEAD MILLS
■ www.arrowheadmills.com

Molasses

Wholesome Sweeteners
■ www.organicsugars.biz

Poppy Seeds, Caraway Seeds, Etc.

SPICELY ORGANICS
■ www.spicely.com

Potato Starch

Potato Starch
ENER-G FOODS
■ www.ener-g.com

Quinoa Flakes

ANCIENT HARVEST QUINOA CORP. QUINOA FLAKES

- www.quinoa.net

Quinoa Flour

ANCIENT HARVEST QUINOA CORP. QUINOA FLOUR

- www.quinoa.net

Rice Bran Oil

California Rice Oil

CALIFORNIA RICE OIL COMPANY

- www.californiariceoil.com

Rice Milk

Pacific Low-Fat Rice Milk, Plain and Vanilla

PACIFIC NATURAL FOODS

- www.pacificfoods.com

Rice Milk Powder

"Better Than Milk" Rice Milk Powder, Original and Vanilla

- www.amazon.com
- www.americanspice.com

Rice Milk Yogurt

Ricera

- www.ricerafoods.com

Sorghum Flour

Bob's Red Mill Sweet Sorghum Flour

- www.glutenfree-supermarket.com

Bob's Red Mill makes tasty sorghum flour, but please note, though it's certified gluten-free, it is not processed in a dedicated nut-free plant—for gluten-free and allergen-free sorghum flour, see below.

Twin Valley Mills Sorghum Flour

- www.twinvalleymills.com

Sprinkles, Etc.

Rainbow and Chocolate Sprinkles

EDWARD AND SONS, LET'S DO ORGANIC "SPRINKELZ"

- www.edwardandsons.com

Various Cookie and Cake Decorative Toppings

INDIA TREE

- www.indiatree.com

Sucanat

Wholesome Sweeteners

- www.organicsugars.biz

SunButter

Sungold SunButter

- www.sunbutter.com

Sungold's allergen statement notes that SunButter is produced in a peanut- and tree nut–free facility, but the facility does process soybeans. If that's a concern, I suggest making your own sunflower seed butter with peanut-free sunflower seeds (see below).

Sunflower Seeds

SunButter's Roasted and Salted Sunflower Seeds

- www.peanutfreeplanet.com

Tapioca Flour (Also Called Tapioca Starch)

Tapioca Flour

ENER-G FOODS

- www.ener-g.com

Unsweetened Baking Chocolate

Vermont Nut Free Chocolates

- www.vermontnutfree.com

Scharffen Berger Unsweetened Home Baking Bars

- www.scharffenberger.com

Unsweetened Cocoa Powder

Vermont Nut Free Chocolates Cocoa Powder

- www.vermontnutfree.com

Hershey's Natural Cocoa Powder

- www.hersheys.com

Vanilla Extract

Meraby's Pure Mexican Vanilla Extract

- www.peanutfreeplanet.com

Madagascar Vanilla Extract from Nielsen-Massey

- www.kingarthurflour.com

Vegetarian Gelatin

Unflavored Jel Dessert
NATURAL DESSERTS
The Nutra Drink Company
- www.nutradrinkco.com

Lieber's Unflavored Jel
- www.veganessentials.com

Xanthan Gum

Ener-G Foods
- www.ener-g.com

Authentic Foods
- www.glutenfree-supermarket.com

HAIN CELESTIAL GROUP/ARROWHEAD MILLS AND SPECTRUM ALLERGEN STATEMENT

"The Hain Celestial Group's labeling declares major allergens (peanuts, soybeans, milk, eggs, fish, crustaceans, tree nuts, and wheat) and we follow the U.S. FDA's regulations. In addition, our labeling always declares gluten-containing ingredients. We recognize the serious nature of the allergen issue and we strive to minimize risk. Both major and minor ingredients of all products, as well as all processing procedures and equipment, are closely scrutinized and all potential allergen issues as determined by the Hain Celestial Group are declared on our labeling. We assure you that strict manufacturing processes and procedures are in place and that all of our manufacturing facilities follow rigid allergen control programs that include staff training, segregation of allergen ingredients, production scheduling, and thorough cleaning and sanitation."

J.M. SMUCKER COMPANY/CRISCO CANOLA OIL ALLERGEN STATEMENT

"All Crisco oils are refined, bleached and deodorized (RBD). This RBD process removes allergenic proteins to the extent that they are not present in detectable amounts in the final product. The FDA considers RBD oils exempt from allergen labeling because they are non-allergenic. Our labeling practices are consistent with FDA labeling regulations and also consistent with FAAN (The Food Allergy & Anaphylaxis Network) and FARRP (University of Nebraska's Food Allergy Research & Resource Program) recommendations for food processors. Although Crisco oils are non-allergenic, validated procedures are used to ensure that cross-contamination does not occur between our products."

HERSHEY'S ALLERGEN STATEMENT

"The Hershey Company strives to provide its consumers with accurate, reliable ingredient statements upon which consumers can make their purchase decision. The Hershey Company has an Allergy Task Force that ensures that the ingredient statements are always accurate, and that any allergen statement placed on the label is understandable. We take food allergies very seriously at Hershey and have strict procedures in place to prevent crossover of allergens into other products that do not contain the allergen. In instances where we have a concern about possible crossover by an allergen we take the added precaution of including an allergy information statement on the label . . . This label provides accurate, current information about all the ingredients in the package."

Allergen-Free/Gluten-Free Online Stores

AllerNeeds
- www.allerneeds.com

Divvies
- www.divvies.com

Edward and Sons Trading Company
- www.edwardandsons.com

Ener-G Foods
- www.ener-g.com

Enjoy Life Foods
- www.enjoylifefoods.com

FAB Snacks
- www.fabsnacks.com

GlutenFree.Com
- www.glutenfree.com

The Gluten-Free Mall
- www.glutenfreemall.com

MotherNature.Com
- www.mothernature.com

Nature's Flavors
- www.naturesflavors.com

Navan Foods, The Allergy Free Food Shop
- www.navanfoods.com

No Nuttin' Foods Inc.
- www.nonuttin.com

Peanut Free Planet
- www.peanutfreeplanet.com

Solutions to Savor
- www.solutionstosavor.com

Vermont Nut Free
- www.vermontnutfree.com

Equipment Sources

Amazon
- www.amazon.com

Bed Bath & Beyond
- www.bedbathandbeyond.com

Bridge Kitchenware
- www.bridgekitchenware.com

Chef's Catalog Co.
- www.chefscatalog.com

King Arthur Flour Tool Shop
- www.kingarthurflour.com

Pastry Chef Central
- www.pastrychef.com

Sur La Table
- www.surlatable.com

Target
- www.target.com

Williams-Sonoma
- www.williams-sonoma.com

Organizations Providing Support and Information for People with Food Allergies and Celiac Disease

Allergic Child
- www.allergicchild.com

Allergic Girl Resources
- www.allergicgirlresources.com

AllergyFree Passport
- www.allergyfreepassport.com

AllergyKids
- www.allergykids.com

AllergyMoms
- www.allergymoms.com

American Academy of Allergy Asthma & Immunology
- www.aaaai.org

American Academy of Pediatrics
- www.aap.org

Anaphylaxis Canada
- www.anaphylaxis.org

Asthma and Allergy Foundation of America
- www.aafa.org

Attention Deficit Disorder Association
- www.add.org

Autism Research Institute
- www.autism.com

Autism Speaks
- www.autismspeaks.org

Celiac Disease Foundation
- www.celiac.org

Celiac Sprue Association
- www.csaceliacs.org

Developmental Delay Resources
- www.devdelay.org

Food Allergy Initiative
- www.foodallergyinitiative.org

Food Allergy & Anaphylaxis Network
- www.foodallergy.org

Gluten-Free Girl
- www.glutenfreegirl.blogspot.com

Gluten Free Life
- www.theglutenfreelife.com

GlutenFree Passport
- www.glutenfreepassport.com

Gluten Intolerance Group of North America
- www.gluten.net

Go Dairy Free
- www.godairyfree.org

International Foundation for Functional Gastrointestinal Disorders
- www.iffgd.org

Jaffe Food Allergy Institute, Mount Sinai School of Medicine
- www.mountsinai.org

Kids with Food Allergies
- www.kidswithfoodallergies.org

University of Chicago Celiac Disease Center
- www.celiacdisease.net

RECIPES MADE WITHOUT REFINED SUGAR

- Morning Glory Muffins, page 24
- Banana Flax Muffins, page 25
- Gingerbread Muffins, page 26
- Buckwheat Apple Muffins, page 32
- Blackberry Quinoa Muffins, page 33
- Baking Powder Biscuits, page 38
- Flax Biscuits, page 39
- Fennel Currant Drop Biscuits, page 40
- Chocolate Zucchini Bread, page 45
- Pumpkin Bread, page 46
- Amaranth Date Bread, page 47
- Gingerbread Boys, page 69
- SunButter Greenies, page 70
- Orange Marmalade Tea Biscuits, page 71
- Quebec Maple Date Cookies, page 79
- SunButter Cupcakes with SunButter Buttercream, page 101
- Chocolate Maple Cupcakes with Rice Milk Chocolate Ganache, page 103
- Golden Agave Cupcakes, page 105
- Carrot Pineapple Bundt Cake with Sucanat Glaze, page 118
- Cranberry Apple Pie (if made with Sucanat Flaky Pie Crust), page 127
- Pumpkin Pie, page 130
- Mixed Berry Crisp, page 145
- Maple Apple Crumble, page 148
- Banana Bread Pudding, page 151
- "Buttermilk" Raisin Bread, page 161
- Buckwheat and Corn Bread, page 163
- Gluten-Free-Beer Bread, page 164
- Rustic Moroccan Loaves, page 165
- Seeded Boule, page 166
- Focaccia, page 168
- Pizza Crust, page 169
- Socca de Nice, page 170
- Matzo, page 171
- Continental Rolls, page 175

INDEX

Note: Page numbers in italics indicate illustrations.

A

Amaranth Date Bread, 47
Apple Brown Betty, 152
Apricot Cornmeal Muffins, 31

B

Baking Powder Biscuits, 38
Banana Bread Pudding, 151
Banana Cake, 114
Banana Cream Pie, 132–133
Banana Flax Muffins, 25
Basic Gluten-Free Flour Mix, 19
Basic Scones, 34
Betties
    about, 123–124
      Apple Brown Betty, 152
      Mango Betty, 153
Blackberry Cobbler, 149
Blackberry Quinoa Muffins, 33
Blueberry Boy Bait, *48, 49*
Blueberry Millet Muffins, 30
Blueberry Pie, 125–126

Bourbon Peach Cobbler, 150
Brandied Peach Tart, 139–140
Breads
    Amaranth Date Bread, 47
    Buckwheat and Corn Bread, 163–164
    "Buttermilk" Raisin Bread, 161–162
    Continental Rolls, 175
    Cornbread Sticks, 171–173
    Dinner Rolls, 174
    Focaccia, 168
    Gluten-Free-Beer Bread, 164
    Matzo, 171
    Pizza Crust, 169
    Potato Bread, 159–160
    Rustic Moroccan Loaves, 165
    Seeded Boule, 166–167
    Socca de Nice, 170
Brownies and Bars
    Chocolate Chunk Blondie Bars, 84, 85
    Chocolate Rice Crispy Treats, 92
    Coconut Chip Bars, 87
    Fudge Brownies, *85*, 86
    Lemon-Lime Squares, 83
Buckles
    about, 123–124
    Cherry Buckle, 154–155

Buckwheat and Corn Bread, 163–164
Buckwheat Apple Muffins, 32
"Buttermilk" Raisin Bread, 161–162

C

Cakes
    Banana Cake, 114
    Carrot Pineapple Bundt Cake with Sucanat
        Glaze, 110
    Chocolate Layer Cake with Dark Chocolate
        Frosting, 106–107
    Christèle's Gâteau au Yaourt (French Yogurt
        Cake), 115
    Classic Yellow Cake, 108
    Lemon Poppy Seed Bundt Cake with Lemon
        Glaze, 117
    Orange Chiffon Cake with Orange Rum Sauce,
        119–120, 121
    Spongecake, 116
    Red Velvet Cake with Velvet Frosting, 109–111
    Strawberry Shortcake with Vegan Whipped
        Topping, 112–113
Chocolate Layer Cake with Dark Chocolate
    Frosting, 106–107
Carrot Ginger Cupcakes with
    Orange Buttercream Frosting, 94–95
Carrot Pineapple Bundt Cake with Sucanat Glaze, 118
Cherry Buckle, 154–155
Cherry Oat Scones, 37
Chocolate Buttercream Frosting, 91
Chocolate Chip Cupcakes, 98, 99–100
Chocolate Chip Frosting, 100
Chocolate Chip Oatmeal Raisin Cookies, 62, 63
Chocolate Chunk Blondie Bars, 84, 85
Chocolate Cupcakes with Chocolate Buttercream
    Frosting, 90–91
Chocolate Layer Cake with Dark Chocolate
    Frosting, 106–107
Chocolate Maple Cupcakes with Rice Milk
    Chocolate Ganache, 103–104

Chocolate Pudding Tart, 134, 135–136
Chocolate Rice Crispy Treats, 82
Chocolate Sandwich Cookies, 56, 57–58, 62
Chocolate Thumbprint Cookies, 60
Chocolate Zucchini Bread, 45
Christèle's Gâteau au Yaourt (French Yogurt
    Cake), 115
Cinnamon Rolls, 41–42, 43
Classic Chocolate Chip Cookies, 54
Classic Crumb Cake, 50–51, 51
Classic Yellow Cake, 108
Cobbler Biscuit Dough, 149
Cobblers
    about, 123
    Blackberry Cobbler, 149
    Bourbon Peach Cobbler, 150
    Cobbler Biscuit Dough, 149
Coconut Chip Bars, 87
Coconut Cupcakes, 96–97
Coconut Frosting, 97
Continental Rolls, 175
Cookies
    about, 53
    Chocolate Chip Oatmeal Raisin Cookies, 62, 63
    Chocolate Chunk Blondie Bars, 84, 85
    Chocolate Rice Crispy Treats, 92
    Chocolate Sandwich Cookies, 56, 57–58, 62
    Chocolate Thumbprint Cookies, 60
    Classic Chocolate Chip Cookies, 54
    Cranberry Chocolate Chip Biscotti. 75–76
    Double Choco Chunk Cookies, 55
    Dutch Cocoa Cookies, 77
    Ginger Snaps, 68
    Gingerbread Boys, 69
    Graham Crackers, 80–81
    Lemon-Lime Squares, 83
    Lemon Madeleines, 72
    Linzer Hearts, 52, 73–74, 74
    Old-Fashioned Oatmeal Lace Cookies, 6
    Orange Marmalade Tea Biscuits, 71
    Orange Spritz Cookies, 65

Cookies, *continued*
    Quebec Maple Date Cookies, 79
    Rolled Brown Sugar Cookies, 66–67
    Russian Rock Cookies, 76
    Snickerdoodles, 59
    SunButter Cupcakes
    SunButterGreenies, 70
    Swedish Cardamom Cookies (Pepper Kakar), 78
    Thin and Crispy Oatmeal Cookies, 61
Cornbread Sticks, 172, *173*
Cornmeal Patê Brisée, 141
Cranberry Apple Pie, 127–128
Cranberry Chocolate Chip Biscotti, 75–76
Crisps
    about, 145
    Mixed Berry Crisp, 145
    Peach Blueberry Crisp, 128, *147*
Crumbles
    Maple Apple Crumble, 148
Cupcakes
    Carrot Ginger Cupcakes with Orange Butter-
        cream Frosting, 97
    Chocolate Chip Cupcakes, 99-100
    Chocolate Cupcakes with Chocolate Butter-
        cream Frosting, 90
    Chocolate Maple Cupcakes with Rice Milk
        Chocolate Ganache, 103–104
    Coconut Cupcakes, 96
    Golden Agave Cupcakes, 105
    SunButter Cupcakes with SunButter Butter-
        cream, *98,*101–102
    Vanilla Cupcakes with Vanilla Frosting, 92–93

D

Dark Chocolate Frosting, 107
Dinner Rolls, 174
Double Choco Chunk Cookies, 55
Double Flaky Pie Crust, 125
Dutch Cocoa Cookies, 77

F

Fennel Currant Drop Biscuits, 40
Flax Biscuits, 39
Focaccia, 168
French Yogurt Cake, 115
Fudge Brownies, *84,* 86

G

Galettes
    Cornmeal Patê Brisée, 141
    Plum Cardamom Galette, 144
    Raspberry Galette with Cornmeal Crust,
        141–142, *143*
Ginger Snaps, 68
Gingerbread Boys, 69
Gingerbread Muffins, 26
Glazed Vanilla Scones, 36
Gluten-Free-Beer Bread, 164
Gluten-Free Bread Flour Mix, 158
Golden Agave Cupcakes, 105
Graham Crackers, 80–81

I

Irish Soda Bread, 44

L

Lemon Madeleines, 72
Lemon-Lime Squares, 83
Lemon Poppy Seed Bundt Cake with Lemon
    Glaze, 117
Linzer Hearts, 52, 73–74

M

Mango Betty, 158
Maple Apple Crumble, 148
Matzo, 171

Mixed Berry Crisp, 146
Mixed Berry Tart, 137
Morning Glory Muffins, 24
Muffins
    Apricot Cornmeal Muffins, 31
    Banana Flax Muffins, 25
    Blackberry Quinoa Muffins, 33
    Blueberry Millet Muffins, 30
    Buckwheat Apple Muffins, 32
    Gingerbread Muffins, 26
    Morning Glory Muffins, 24
    Orange Cranberry Muffins, 28, 29
    Plum Coffee Cake Muffins, 27

O

Old-Fashioned Oatmeal Lace Cookies, 64
Orange Buttercream Frosting, 95
Orange Chiffon Cake with Orange Rum Sauce,
    119–120, 121
Orange Cranberry Muffins, 28, 29
Orange Marmalade Tea Biscuits, 71
Orange Rum Sauce, 120
Orange Scones, 35
Orange Spritz Cookies, 65

P

Pastry Custard, 137
Peach Blueberry Crisp, 146, 147
Pear Blackberry Tart, 140
Pepper Kakar (Swedish Cardamom Cookies),
    78, 79
Pies
    about, 123
    Banana Cream Pie, 132-133
    Blueberry Pie, 125-126
    Double Flaky Pie Crust, 125
    Cranberry Apple Pie, 127-128, 129
    Pumpkin Pie, 130-132

Single Flaky Pie Crust, 132
    Single Flaky Sucanat Pie Crust, 130
Pizza Crust, 169
Plum Cardamom Galette, 144
Plum Coffee Cake Muffins, 27
Potato Bread, 159–160
Prune Purée, 9
Puddings
    about, 123
    Banana Bread Pudding, 151
Pumpkin Bread, 46
Pumpkin Pie, 130–131

Q

Quebec Maple Date Scones, 79

R

Raspberry Galette with Cornmeal Crust,
    141–142, 143
Red Velvet Cake with Velvet Frosting, 109–111
Rice Milk Chocolate Ganache, 103–104
Rice Milk Glaze, 42
Rolled Brown Sugar Cookies, 66–67
Rolls
    Continental Rolls, 175
    Dinner Rolls, 174
Russian Rock Cookies, 76
Rustic Moroccan Loaves, 165

S

Scones
    Basic Scones, 34
    Cherry Oat Scones, 37
    Glazed Vanilla Scones, 36
    Orange Scones, 35
Seeded Boule, 166–167
Shortbread Tart Crust, 136

Single Flaky Pie Crust, 132
Single Flaky Sucanat Pie Crust, 130
Socca de Nice, 170
Snickerdoodles, 59
Spongecake, 116
Strawberry Shortcake with Vegan Whipped
    Topping, 112–113
Sucanat Glaze, 118
SunButter Buttercream, 102
SunButter Cupcakes with SunButter Buttercream,
    101–102
SunButter Greenies, 70
Swedish Cardamom Cookies (Peppar Kakar), 78
Sweet Potato Purée, 9

T

Tapioca, about instant, 9
Tarts
    Brandied Peach Tart, 138–139
    Chocolate Pudding Tart, *134*, 135–136
    Mixed Berry Tart, 137
    Pastry Custard, 137
    Pear Blackberry Tart, 140
    Shortbread Tart Crust, 136
Thin and Crispy Oatmeal Cookies, 61

V

Vanilla Cupcakes with Vanilla Frosting, 92–93
Vanilla Frosting, 93
Vanilla Glaze, 36
Vegan Whipped Topping, 113
Velvet Frosting, 110, *111*

W

White Icing, 66–67

ACKNOWLEDGMENTS

Thanks to my excellent family allergists Robert Eitches, MD, and Maxine Baum, MD; to my agent Mitchell S. Waters at Curtis Brown Ltd. for his belief in this project; to David Stefanou for telling me it was time to do a second book; to my fabulous editor at Ten Speed/Celestial Arts, Melissa Moore; to Chugrad McAndrews for his exquisite photographs; to Karen Shinto for her awesome food styling, and to both Karen and her brother Barry for their expert baking; and to Leigh Noe for her prop styling that was my aesthetic dream come true.

Big huge thanks to my favorite taste-testers, my two sons Lennon and Monte, and my husband Adam; to my taste-tester friends Lilly Falakshahi (the coffee goddess of Laurel Canyon) and Spike Stewart; Amy Hobgood, Rachel, David, Mia, and Jacob Ronn; Deirdre Moncy and Dennis Mount; Micah Schraft; Sara Gomez; the kids at Wonderland Avenue Elementary; Erika Carpenter Rich; Mark, Katie, Rives, Harry, and Charlie Cowen; and Christèle Albright. I am extremely grateful to my amazing field testers who tested out the recipes for me: Nathan Dean, Liz Benjamin, and Henry Smith; Willie, Kay, Ella, and Winston Wisely; Tatyana Yassukovich, Ben, Maude, Leo, Nelly, Lucy, and Boris Duke; Michele Conklin, Sophia, Enzo, and Joe Montrone; Walker and Correia Borba; Talulah Brown, Brandi, Marc, Malin, Henry, and Domenic Smith; Jacqueline, Michael, Elia, and Noah Rosner; Mimi McCracken, Joel, and Solly Plotch; Ellen Genco; Jeannine Russo, Rob Canter, and their food-allergic daughter Sofia: and Beth Lein. You all rocked it! Thanks to my adorable cousin Jaz Daniels whom you see eating the sweets in this book and to my cousin Ila Deiss for allowing me to use her daughter as a model. Thanks to my father Eric, mother Susanna, brothers Dylan and Judah, and sister-in-law Thanya for their support and advice. And special thanks to Jeannie Kang, my acupuncturist, who allowed me to finish this book by curing the acute neck pain I was suffering from after so many hours stooped over at the counter and sitting at the computer.